The Hybrid Entrepreneur

The Hybrid Entrepreneur

A Novel Career in Science and Business

Kevin J. Scanlon, PhD
CEO
International BioScience

BUSINESS EXPERT PRESS

Leader in applied, concise business books

The Hybrid Entrepreneur: A Novel Career in Science and Business

Cover design by Klassic Designs

Interior design by Exeter Premedia Services Private Ltd., Chennai, India

First published in 2023 by
Business Expert Press, LLC
222 East 46th Street, New York, NY 10017
www.businessexpertpress.com

ISBN-13: 978-1-63742-444-5 (paperback)
ISBN-13: 978-1-63742-445-2 (e-book)

Business Expert Press Entrepreneurship and Small Business Management Collection

First edition: 2023

10 9 8 7 6 5 4 3 2 1

Description

Do you want to start your own company?

This book describes the management expertise, organizational skills, and vocabulary necessary to be a successful entrepreneur based on the author's academic and business career.

This book discusses the following:

- What are the successful characteristics of an inventor, an entrepreneur, and a CEO?
- Understanding the vocabulary of the entrepreneur's ecosystem.
- What are the evaluation criteria for the team, product, business model, and exit plan?
- Do consumers need or want your product?
- How to create the story that will fit the right investor for funding?
- Understanding the investor evaluation and screening process.

Readers will learn how to ask the right questions to build a strong ecosystem with service providers, customers, and investors.

If you want to be an entrepreneur, read this book. It is about the author's personal experiences as a scientist, an inventor, an entrepreneur, a CEO, and an investor.

Keywords

entrepreneur; startups; investors; incubators; funding process; legal issues; service providers; business strategy

Contents

Testimonials

"*I would highly recommend this book to anyone who is curious about entrepreneurship. The book provides comprehensive knowledge about the venture creation process. Coming from a healthcare background, I had no prior business knowledge. However, I thoroughly enjoyed reading the book and learned so much from it. I believe that everyone can be an entrepreneur if they have the right resource, and this book is the perfect starting point.*"—**Thy Nguyen, Doctor of Pharmacy student, School of Pharmacy, Bouve College of Health Sciences, Northeastern University**

"*This is a must-read for budding entrepreneurs. Working in healthcare, I always wanted to address significant unmet needs and inefficiencies in the industry by taking an entrepreneurial approach, but I frankly didn't know where to start. Like most students, I tried learning as much as possible about entrepreneurship through various online resources and talking to mentors. Still, I never truly felt that I was getting it (seeing the whole picture). Then I read* The Hybrid Entrepreneur, *which gave me a unique bird's-eye view of the venture creation/building process and detailed the caveats to consider along the journey in an easily digestible way. So, I highly recommend this book, especially for budding entrepreneurs.*"—**Joon Seok Lee, Doctor of Pharmacy student, School of Pharmacy, Bouve College of Health Sciences, Northeastern University**

"*This book is a great help for entrepreneurs and investors.*"—**Eyal Geffen, Managing Partner, Sky Ventures Group**

"*Kevin Scanlon has written the requisite book for every scientific entrepreneur with a vision of a product and commercial success. The entrepreneur has the required tenacity for the vision but understanding the business/commercial aspects will either make or break the aspiring entrepreneur. Scanlon repeatedly states a mentor is critical, it's true and I concur.* The Hybrid Entrepreneur *should be required reading in any MBA entrepreneurial program. Scientific entrepreneurship is an interesting breed, brilliant inventions that can become game changers in industry. A step-by-step outline for essential, capitalization, commercialization will absolutely determine if the vision becomes actuality. The business tenets discussed in the book will help the scientist to transition to a businessperson who can discuss ROI one minute and the next molecular genetics diagnostics."*—**Lawrence A. Rheins, PhD, Inventor, Founder and CEO, DermTech International**

"The Hybrid Entrepreneur *is a must read for any scientist seeking to commercialize their innovation. Moving from bench to boardroom is much harder than the other direction. The hybrid scientist/businessperson has difficulty in that there are no specific solutions to each issue that arises until a solution is tried. Dr. Scanlon demonstrates the many methods to reduce the uncertainty surrounding the hybrid entrepreneur and guide them through better decision making."*—**Mark Lieberman, Chief Startup Officer, OSU Advantage Accelerator, Oregon State University**

Acknowledgments

My Family: Alysa, Kara, Lauren, Maeve, Quinn, and Damian

My Students for their interesting questions

My Science Mentors
Dr. J. R. Bertino (Yale Medical School)
Dr. J. Holland (Mt. Sinai Medical School)
Dr. M. Dietal (Charite Hospital, Berlin, Germany)

My Business Mentors
Dr. D. Stringfellow (Schering AG/Berlex)
M. Lieberman (Pasadena Angels Investment Group)
A. Schneider (Pasadena Angels Investment Group)

My Legal Mentors
J. G. Sheldon (Pasadena Angels Investment Group)
D. Thompson (Pasadena Angels Investment Group)
S. M. Honig (Duane Morris)

Introduction

If it were easy to be an entrepreneur, everybody would do it.
—Robert Kiyosaki

In my experience, companies fail for two main reasons: The team dynamics change as the company grows and/or lack of money. This book will address these key business topics and additional issues typically faced by new ventures. First, we will evaluate commercially successful companies that took their concept to market. Next, we learn the vocabulary of the investor, customer, and management team to maximize the successful process of taking a concept to market. The questions we will address are the following: What are the skills and tools required for starting a new venture? What are the characteristics of an inventor, an entrepreneur, and a CEO? Do consumers need your product? How can you create a story that will interest investors? *The Hybrid Entrepreneur* should help you build you a strong foundation for your company.

This book is divided into five parts. We will review the essential elements needed for your new venture: a team, the product, a business plan, the business model, and the ecosystem to grow your new business. The team will be defined by the type of leader required for the stage of the company. The team requires certain skills and domain experience to run the enterprise. An evaluation of the organizational structure and the appropriate board for the company will be examined. The problem and the solution should be easily explained to either a customer or an investor. The product must address the needs of the customer and market. The product should have acquired legal protections to satisfy the needs of the investors. The legal protections should create a strong picket fence around the product to keep the competitors out of the market. Conversely, the protections should be strong enough to encourage the competitor to buy the product rights. The business plan should validate the target customer needs. The product should be identified in a growing niche market that can produce strong growth of revenues. The business model should demonstrate a value proposition to the customer and have a strong sales cycle with multiple revenue streams of income. The final section will evaluate the contribution to making a successful venture with help from incubators, attorneys, and investors. The success of a company is measured by the return on investment at the exit of the company.

In addition, we will analyze these five parts from the point of view of an entrepreneur, a customer, and an investor. The challenge for the entrepreneur is to link their transformational idea to a significant problem. Ironically, solving a small problem can sometimes lead to a solution to a bigger problem. In nature, an organism's ability to adapt to a changing environment allows it to survive. Products need the ability to adapt to the customer's needs to grow in their commercial environment. Adapting to the ecosystem will allow the product or species to grow. This book will help you find the right ecosystem. The success of your product is dependent on your network of entrepreneurs, customers, investors, and service providers.

The *Hybrid Entrepreneur* can help you:

- Learn the skills to build a strong team.
- Learn the vocabulary of the CEO, the customer, and the investor.
- Learn how to do an investor pitch and an investor presentation.
- Create a useful customer survey.
- Define your business plan.
- Understand the investor company evaluation process.
- Understand due diligence and the term sheet conditions.
- Find where to meet investors.
- Identify the personality/domain expertise fit between entrepreneurs and investors.

If I had known these fundamentals before starting my business career, my journey might have taken an easier path. My personal experiences as an inventor, entrepreneur, and investor are described herein. I hope my experiences as a hybrid entrepreneur will help clarify the different paths ahead of you.

CHAPTER 1

The Three Legs of the Venture Stool

The three legs of the venture stool are entrepreneurs, customers, and investors. They are the basis for a convergent ecosystem. Their relationships test the economic viability of new products. A successful entrepreneur thrives in this dynamic ecosystem. Novel products should meet the needs or adapt to the wants of the customer. The investor will bring their resources and network to help make a profitable company.

The information presented herein is from my career experiences as an inventor, entrepreneur, and investor. The process of developing a successful product requires creativity and execution. Creating a concept, making a minimum viable product (MVP), demonstrating customer demand, and finding investors to fund the company are a complex endeavor. Success depends on a supportive business environment. Investors can provide more than just the money for the company; they can use their experience and network to help the team. Customers can enjoy new features to the product to outpace the competition. The entrepreneur will benefit from this supportive network.

Conversely, most companies fail by running out of money or by having team members whose expectations change. The team may not evolve with the growth of the company. The customer may lose interest in your product for a better solution. The investor knows getting a product to market takes twice as long and twice as much money as projected by the entrepreneur. This is an optimistic view of the investor. Most new ventures will require bridge funding to survive.

In evolution, organisms with unique properties often survive in specific environments. The changing environment stimulates new adoption processes (mutations) in the organisms. Adapting to a changing business environment can produce novel products that will survive in an evolving and changing commercial ecosystem. The business culture tests entrepreneurial ideas to see if they are economically viable. This business ecosystem involves individuals with the support of financial organizations and professional resources. Successful products generate successful entrepreneurs who can generate successful networks. The solution for successful companies is to create an educated and collaborative community for spinning out technology.

There are at least two challenges facing the entrepreneur: finding a good mentor and trusting the business community. Learning to trust the business community is particularly difficult for some scientists to learn. They need a good mentor if they want to start a new enterprise.

The Technologist and/or Businessperson

It is easier to train a scientist to learn business than a businessperson to learn the science.

—Dr. Dale Stringfellow,
CEO, Berlex

A technologist can move from the laboratory bench to the business world but usually with difficulty. The business process, the business vocabulary, and the team dynamics are a challenge for scientists. They come from a different culture. The inventor needs to become an entrepreneur and attract a strong business team. But most companies need both technology and business expertise. The scientist has a strong knowledge of the product, while the partner can have a strong knowledge of the business process to make money. The company needs both these unique skills to work together. If the company lacks the skills in either area, then this adventure may be doomed. We have seen this failure in many companies that we have screened in our investment groups.

The Team

If the entrepreneur has good personal skills, they can find a supportive team. The team must be comfortable with the challenges of the day-to-day operations. Scientists are notorious about their passion but sometimes to a fault. Scientists love to talk science, can sometimes go on for hours, but can be challenged by social settings. They may lack the skills necessary to be an effective extrovert in business. The business culture likes to get to the point quickly and directly, no nonsense. An entrepreneur with both skill sets is rare but does occur. A *hybrid entrepreneur* (a scientist/ businessperson) may find the challenges even more difficult. They have training in both scientific research and business expertise. These scientists are rare and have unique life experiences. The challenge is to manage their educational training internally. Unfortunately, it has not been done well in most cases, but it has worked for some scientists. Reconciling these two cultures in one person is difficult but it can be done. There are several examples of academic professors becoming successful entrepreneurs. These entrepreneurs were able to identify what the customers needed. They were able to make a product that was faster, cheaper, and better than what was currently available on the market. They also provided good value and product reliability to ensure customer retention.

The Product

The company needs to test the product by third party validation and ensure it is a significant improvement over the competition. Additional diligence by the investor will be the type of legal protections of the product. The concept is reduced to practice. There are barriers to entry with the competing product. The legally protected product can be licensed or codeveloped without fear from the competition. Investors look for sustainable advantage over the competition with disruptive technology.

The Customer

If the product does not adapt to the changes in their market, the product will die.

—Dr. Kevin Scanlon

The entrepreneur needs to clearly define the product for the customer. This can be achieved through the help of an effective customer survey. A clear result of the survey would validate the target customer or require a pivot of the product features or a new target customer. The survey should confirm the ability of the customer to buy the product and that it is better than the competition. For the product to create a beachhead market, it must be better, faster, and cheaper than the competition and take away market share from competitors. Investors will evaluate the customer and market from the point of view of growth, market size, competition, and value proposition to the customer.

The Investor

Investors would rather support a strong team with a weak product than a strong product and a weak team.

—Angel Investor Philosophy

The entrepreneur needs the investors' domain knowledge of the product, customer/market, their mentoring skills, and their network. Conversely, investors want to see a balanced team that can take a concept to market. The investor needs to get a good return on investment (ROI). Quick ROI allows for timely reinvestments in other new opportunities. This also prevents funding from being tied up for long periods of time.

The Pasadena Angels are a respected and accredited group of investors in Southern California. As a member of this group, I have seen that during the screening process we can receive about 25 to 50 company applications per month; we screen around 8 of these companies and typically have 4 present to the membership on a monthly basis. Roughly only one out of four of these companies moves through due diligence and receives a term sheet, a document which outlines the terms of investment and funding being offered. We also do "follow-on funding or bridge funding" for our portfolio companies. We fund about 25 companies annually out of about 600 screened applications.

Investors need confidence in the team to fund a company. The team should have a strong track record of performance with their product, customer, and market. A strong team can weather the ups and downs of a company's growth. A great product can easily fail with a weak team. Conversely, a strong team can pivot if the product does not match the customer's needs. Some of the questions an inventor should ask before starting this adventure include: Is the founder a scientist or a businessperson? Can the inventor learn the skills of business and grow into an entrepreneur/CEO? Will the company be supported by a strong team and ecosystem? The investor is always looking to be part of a successful team.

Conclusion

Success has many fathers, but failure is an orphan.

—John F. Kennedy

The convergence of a business culture with a technology product may vary regionally. However, the business principals of starting a new venture remain the same anywhere. Strong business mentors and a supportive ecosystem are the key to enhancing the success rate of new ventures. We will look at the components that can make a successful company. Hopefully, these insights will improve the quality and success of new ventures.

Reflections on the Issues Addressed in This Section

- Does the company have the right product?
- Does the customer know the company and want your product?
- Does the investor want to invest in your company?

PART 1

The Team

Chapter 2. The Leader

An inventor, entrepreneur, or CEO

Startup challenges: Do you have a flash of inspiration followed by a handful of nagging doubts? You need to be honest with yourself; conviction is important, but blind conviction is also dangerous.

Chapter 3. The Management Team

The team will be defined by the type of leader you are and what is required for the different stages of this enterprise. The team requires certain skills and domain experience to run the company. The organizational structure and board composition for the company are critical for success.

Chapter 4. The Company

Get the right people on the right bus and in the right seat.

—James C. Collins

The success of a company is measured by customer satisfaction for the product, the ROI to the investors, and a healthy culture of the company.

To be a successful entrepreneur, remember The Rule of Three:
Network, network, and network
Practice, practice, and practice
Quality, quality, and quality

CHAPTER 2

The Leader

Your Character is your Destiny.
— Words over the entrance at Delphi in Greece.

Odysseus is a good role model for being an entrepreneur. His 20-year journey from Ithaca to Troy and home was an epic journey described by Homer. To survive his travels around the Mediterranean, he relied on his intelligence, determination, and cunningness. Once arriving at home, he had to deal with the greedy suitors camped in his home. He was able to overcome all these challenges to rejoin his beloved wife, Penelope. His journey was filled with many twists and turns. The career of an entrepreneur also can be filled with many twists and turns.

The leader in a new venture requires a reputation of high legal and moral standards. The legal test is to stay out of court. But there is another test. While certain behaviors may not be illegal, they could be immoral. Would you survive an immoral disclosure in the newspaper? This is often referred to as "the Warren Buffet Test." Reputations take years to make but can be lost in minutes by inappropriate behavior.

Who Are You?

Are you an inventor, an entrepreneur, or a CEO? There are several growth stages for a new venture. The leader can be an inventor, an entrepreneur, or a CEO. There are many types of *inventors*. But the challenge for the inventor is to translate their innovative concepts into products. A new startup requires a novel product to solve an important problem. In contrast, the *entrepreneur* is required to create a dynamic team to bring a product to market. The company is dependent on the skills of the team. Can they reach their customer and get traction in the market with sales of the product? The entrepreneur will also need to attract investors. Finally, establishing a mature company will require a seasoned manager. The CEO is required to manage the team, create the organizational structure, report to a board of directors, and maximize the value of the company. All three jobs require different skills, experience, and good mentors. Each stage of growth is critical for the success of the company.

The leader should be able to clearly articulate the unique assets of the company. You may need to explain why you first became interested in the problem. What did you find when researching the product? What assumptions did you make regarding the solution? What are your unanswered questions? What issues keep you up at night?

The Inventor

The inventor's skills are innovation and the ability to create a solution to an existing problem. Inventors are self-confident, have high energy, and can easily set milestones and goals. They are committed to the challenge of bringing their concepts to a product. An interesting question for the inventor is: How did they come up with the solution? Why does the inventor think the problem is so important? Does the product solve an important problem that can be legally protected from competitors? A customer wants a product and not a concept, a prototype, a minimum viable product (MVP), or a perfect product. Will your product disrupt the market? Will the customer buy the product?

I personally have never set out to be an entrepreneur or have a business career. I was very happy working at the lab bench. It never occurred to me that my research was patentable. However, my research generated several patents and a pharmaceutical executive suggested that I publish my work in a top science journal and patent the research. This led me to work with my first patent attorney. He was exceptional—a great teacher—and gave me a strong foundation in patent law. He had clarity of thought and a logic in writing patents. I got the business bug from him. I then followed a path into the pharmaceutical industry where I worked with that same pharmaceutical executive.

That was an eye-opening experience. I was no longer living in an ivory tower. My career path would never again be a straight line. I have enjoyed these twists and turns in my career.

If you want to go from an inventor to an entrepreneur, it will be a lifetime of learning. These challenging new environments got me out of my comfort zone. The Jesuit philosophy calls it "A Thirst for Knowledge." Learning requires taking a risk and having good mentors. The mentors can also be your safety net. Weak mentors can also show you what not to do.

In my career experience, I moved from pure research on messenger RNA to using ribozyme technology to understand oncogenes and doing gene therapy. I went from the lab bench into the pharmaceutical industry and then into the investment community in a period of 10 years. I learned a new vocabulary, worked with interesting personalities, and was introduced to different business cultures. This adventure was filled with challenges. In addition, I worked with several outstanding students and helped facilitate the creation of their companies.

Inventor to Entrepreneur

Starting a company can be a risky and painful endeavor. The progress to achieve milestones and goals can be slow and painful. Failure is always around the corner, but it is important to stay calm. The character of the entrepreneur is a good reflection of the potential success of their new venture. The investor will carefully evaluate the behavior and skills of an entrepreneur. Investors observe how they deal with the challenges of their company. I have had a few failures transitioning from inventor to entrepreneur. In my startup companies, I have had to deal with difficult team dynamics, funding issues, and problematic scientists. These were good but painful learning experiences. Writing this book has helped clarify my experience as an inventor, an entrepreneur, and an investor. The skills that make you a successful inventor may not be the same skills needed to be a successful entrepreneur or CEO.

The Entrepreneur

An entrepreneur's most important skill is their ability to tolerate uncertainty. They persist at solving problems, learn from their failures, deal with constructive criticism, and learn to use the company resources/

funding wisely. The entrepreneur will need to form a strong team, create a product better than the competition, and attract investors. The customer will want to buy their product. They will understand the solution to the problem. The investor will need to understand the product and whether the market is large enough to make money.

The founder of a company is an optimist; they must be patient, be hardworking, and have good social skills. They must be decisive when moving their concept to market. Ambiguity occurs at every turn. Scientists have a passion for their research; sometimes that can be good in helping them overcome obstacles. At other times, it can be a fatal flaw. The ability to bounce back from critical setbacks ensures the entrepreneur/businessperson success in their long-term vision and goals.

Entrepreneurs are often serial entrepreneurs. After starting several companies, the founder develops a strong set of skills that are effective in running a company. Conversely, what made them successful in one company may not be the skills to make them successful in the next company. They may face different issues and personnel problems.

The entrepreneur's success will also be dependent on the experience of the team, educational experience, and personal passion for their product. This journey is surrounded by risks, but you can learn from previous mistakes and that knowledge can serve you well in the next company.

Entrepreneurs need to have a thick skin and a good sense of humor to help overcome the roller coaster ride. Business can be a high-pressure environment with important decisions that need to be made quickly. In business, rarely do you have the time to sleep on an important decision. In contrast, academic decisions can take weeks, months, or even years. A good entrepreneur should question most information; there is value in being a bit skeptical and savvy.

As a founder, you need to question yourself constantly. Naively believing everything is a fatal flaw. Scientists are good at perseverance; there are very few researchers that get instant gratification from their experiments. Most scientists are good with data and getting to the facts and not letting their emotions overrule their objectivity. There is no substitute for hard work and staying focused on the present in both life and work. But without curiosity, imagination, and fortitude, you cannot change the world.

The Types of Entrepreneurs

There are several types of products managed by entrepreneurs. There are technology companies with products. Investors prefer these companies because the product is protected with intellectual property (IP). If the company goes bankrupt, the investor will be protected by the company patents and recover some of their investments. Other types of products include lifestyle companies, socially minded nonprofit companies, and family businesses. This book will focus on the technology startups and even corporate spinoffs with new product lines because of my background and knowledge of the investment community. The principals and skills of being an entrepreneur for any of the companies mentioned before are the same. The ecosystem with its service providers and investors can provide a similar path to success for service startups, social ventures, and family-managed businesses.

The Hybrid Entrepreneur

One ass cannot ride two horses.

—Dr. W. Rhode,
Polish scientist

Can you manage the ambiguity of both science and business? The scientist wants to commercialize their discoveries. But their culture, training, and education are different from the business culture. For one person to span both disciplines requires an understanding of the language, personalities, and strength or limits of the team's interactions. This is the struggle of the hybrid entrepreneur and the team. How this culture is balanced in the team can determine the success or failure of a venture. Scientific founders may not have all the answers as described above but honesty is critical for developing a relationship with both the customer and the investor. If done right, the business process and the scientific process are open ended, interactive, and disciplined. The challenge for a hybrid entrepreneur is overcoming their academic (education) culture and learning the new vocabulary and mindset of a businessperson.

Scientist–Inventor–Entrepreneur–Businessperson

Business decisions sometimes need to be made quickly and are more like driving a Porsche in fifth gear down the Alps. In contrast, academic decisions can take longer and are more like driving a Volkswagen in the first gear up the Alps.

The science-trained entrepreneur has a strong background in problem solving. The product must be novel and better than the competition. If the product requires U.S. Food and Drug Administration (FDA)/Regulatory approval, then the team needs regulatory experience to manage the approval process.

The science-trained entrepreneur with business experience needs to understand the customer and market. If the product needs to change or the target customer or market niche needs to be modified, then the team needs to pivot. Investors look for the product's go-to-market plan. How does the plan fit into the business model? Do the financials match the business plan and go-to-market strategy? Financial management is critical in a money crisis. Financial issues are one of the main reasons companies fail in the early stages.

A Successful Entrepreneur

Keep Calm and Carry On.
> —Motivational poster produced by The British Ministry of
> Information,1939

The leader needs to communicate their vision clearly. Your company's message needs be memorable, your product should solve an important problem, your customer needs the product, the market is growing, and the business model is good for you and the investor. Your story should be interesting enough that investors follow up with questions. You will have hooked them by giving them more details about your company.

Business CEO Versus Scientist CEO

A science team is very different from a business team in terms of goals, timelines, and milestones. A principal investigator is a world authority on their scientific subject; in contrast, a CEO is a generalist and the team members are the experts (product, legal, financial, and market). The scientist's goals are grant funding, publications, and academic awards. In contrast, business goals are getting products to market and a good exit for the company. This will ensure a timely ROI for investors and a good bonus.

The CEO

A skilled CEO is a good general manager who understands the technology, product development, customer, and market. The CEO relies on a strong diverse team. They have an advisory board of experts that talk straight and listen to the problems carefully. A successful CEO can supply excellent rewards to the team and investors by creating a profitable exit. They can scale the business to make a successful product which meets the needs of the customer. The customer will buy the product because it is better and cheaper than what's currently being offered by competitors. The investor can see a sale of the company with a solid ROI.

The CEO skill set for an early-stage company is very different than a Fortune 500 company. Both ventures will have some fundamental common business processes. As investors, we have seen managers from large corporations enter the startup community with a new product or technology. The corporate CEO has difficulty transitioning from a strong supportive environment with administrators and large budgets for research, travel, and entertainment funds. The startup environment requires management to do everything themselves within a very tight budget. The company CEO manages a small team and serves as a board advisor. These boards can include investors. They will set the company goals and milestones. The CEO will execute the business plan with their team. Growing the business is the key to the success of the CEO with a good ROI to the investors. Making money from the new product is essential.

A strong CEO has the ability to embrace change. The job comes with a high level of ambiguity including the uncertainty in the business climate, plans for mergers or acquisitions, new competitors entering the market, and regulatory challenges. Embracing and managing change allows for continued success. The CEO should be a domain matter expert in their business. The CEO needs to understand industry levers, develop strong relationships, and know how to increase the value in their given market. The CEO should be able to effectively use analytics to drive their business strategy. They need to fully understand the business. They will also use metrics to verify and monitor activities to adjust strategy and drive for the right results. They are agile managers; they navigate situations by building strong teams that work collaboratively and get results. They focus on finances, not just spending and income, but also margin, profit, and growth, and then use the information to drive business decisions.

Conversely, the CEO must recognize several traps that can ruin their company. These include getting too comfortable, not hiring the strongest candidates, not managing the strengths and weaknesses of employees, not improving the product or team, and taking employees for granted.

Investor Evaluation of the Company Leader

A smooth working team is essential for creating investor interest in your company. I have managed a dysfunctional team. We had a team member with unrealistic expectations of the company. They would not listen or accept any suggestions from investors or an acquiring company on the valuation of the company. There was nothing we could do that would convince this person that they were off base. They ultimately destroyed the company.

Investors know that there are several fatal mistakes founders can make with their new ventures. Scientists and engineers want to make their science/product perfect. But investors just want their products in the market, selling as soon as possible.

Investors want to fund a company with a good product that will give a good ROI. They do not want to fund a science project. Can you make money with the current business model and the go-to-market plan to support the sale of your product?

The financials sometimes answer one of the most important questions for the investors. The company needs to present a clear and realistic budget. Another requirement from investors is the use of their funds. Occasionally, the CEO can have unrealistic salary requirements or a rich equity position in the company. Sometimes the company has onerous contracts, or the capitalization table (Cap Table) shows anomalies or a board member with financial issues. I'm aware of one company that investors were very interested in funding because it had a novel product for the building industry. The problem was the CEO needed half of the funding to pay off a large family loan ($500,000). The deal did not go forward with the investors.

The Company Pitch for the Investor in 60 to 120 Seconds

The entrepreneur needs to explain their company and product quickly to the investor. The pitch, with passion, should be clear and address key issues for the investor. The following questions should be addressed in less than two minutes.

- What is the problem?
- Why is your solution best?
- Is the product protected and what is the stage of development?
- Does the customer need your product and is the market growing?
- Is the team experienced?
- What are your financial needs?
- Is your road map clear?

If the entrepreneur can communicate this information clearly and passionately, the investor will follow up with more questions. This is always a good sign for moving forward. But this process takes practice, practice, and more practice. I've taught courses on how to make funding pitches, and students typically spend six to eight weeks refining their presentations. The presentations improve dramatically week to week. There is a confidence factor in practicing and refining the pitch.

A successful pitch is about finding the right fit between the company and the investor. Do your company visions match the investors' interests? If not, keep trying.

Conclusion

This section defined the role of a leader in the company. Are you an inventor, an entrepreneur, or a CEO businessperson?

Each type of leader has certain types of skills to offer the company. The customer is looking for a product with a beneficial value. The investor is looking for a strong investment. The reputation of the company is essential for market growth. The company's reputation will define their success. Will they pass the newspaper test? Can the leader help the company grow and be successful with the right customer and market? Or will you need to pivot so the investors will be interested in your business?

Scientists who want to start companies based on their technology may become hybrid entrepreneurs. The process of moving from inventor to entrepreneur to CEO is complex and requires business veterans that can mentor the founders. By understanding the business landscape, personalities, and vocabulary, this journey can be made easier. Understanding this network is critical for building a successful business. Your leadership of the company is characterized by your reputation.

Creating a company often requires its founder to be an iconoclast, an outsider who challenges popular beliefs and traditions. This is the living legacy of explorers, dreamers, and pioneers who changed the world. Unfortunately, pioneers can take a lot of arrows in their backs. The best entrepreneurs can solve big questions of climate change, hunger, and disease as well as providing innovation. Without their curiosity, imagination, and fortitude, humankind will be limited in every respect.

That which does not kill us makes us stronger.
—Friedrich Nietzsche

Reflections on the Issues Addressed in This Section

- Does the company have the right leadership?
- Does the customer know the company and leader's reputation?
- Does the investor want to invest in this leader?

CHAPTER 3

The Management Team

The Introduction

The entrepreneur needs to attract a quality team with an experienced track record. This helps to be coachable, have dynamic interactions, and be able to share a passion for the product.

The Team Leader

The leader should be able to explain the importance of the technology to the investors. The investor should be able to understand the technology. If not, sometimes the chief scientific officer can help explain the product in more detail to the domain expert in the investment group. The novelty of the product needs to be carefully explained to investors in its simplest form. The job of the company is to educate the investor domain experts. They can then educate the investors in understanding the company and the product.

An inventor may just want to tinker with the prototype and make it perfect. The investor just wants a product to sell. The inventor may not want to be the company CEO; inventors often lack business experience, the ability to build a team, or get the product to market. The investors may not be interested in financially supporting research activity. The inventor may also want to be the chairperson of the scientific advisory board.

Conversely, the entrepreneur may not be the creator of the technology but is the person to build the team. The job of the entrepreneur is to get funding for the company. They can get the prototype to market and help build a company advisory board. They can create a diverse team with different experiences focused on the same goal.

The ideal team should also include women. Studies have shown an increase in success for companies with women on the team and boards. Their ability to look at the problem differently and their attention to detail are critical for rounding out the team and achieving the company goals.

A strong team has a track record of experience with the product and a knowledge of the customer and market. There are several well-known examples of good team synergy and successful companies. If you think of successful products, they have successful teams. An experienced team with domain knowledge can foresee problems before they happen. The investors know the behavior of good teams after years of watching presentations. Complementary skills allow individual strengths to overcome weaknesses and create a synergistic team. Investors can use their network to also help fill in the gaps on the team. They can mentor the entrepreneur, but investors really want a knowledgeable CEO. The investors are more comfortable with a seasoned businessperson managing a company through product development, team dynamics, financing, and building an advisory board.

The team needs to know the technology, but the inventor may want to perfect the product. The CEO needs drive, energy, self-confidence, and a long-term involvement in the company as a source of institutional knowledge. The entrepreneur can build a team, get the product to market, learn from their failures, build a board, and get initial investors. The CEO gets direction from the board; sets goals, milestones, and timelines; scales the product; defines the customer/market; and helps prepare an exit strategy for the company.

The Team

In the team ecosystem, cultural differences, gender differences, educational backgrounds, and different languages are important diversity elements. When mixed well, they can help achieve the company's goals. These differences can also make or break a company.

The team leader, or CEO, has the characteristics of knowing the business and has the big picture of the customer, market, the financials, and vision for the critical path forward. The team leader must have good empathy for managing the process from concept to product. In addition, analytic intelligence (IQ/EQ) and critical thinking are important for the success of the team. The company must have transparency regarding stock, bonuses, and budget. Individual success, domain expert knowledge, self-sufficiency, funded research programs, and academic awards can also bring critical tools to the team. Other team members include:

- **The Attorney**. The product needs protection and the company needs to be legally created.
- **The Technologist.** The chief science officer needs attention to detail to get the concept to product.
- **Product Development**. The novel product must have a clear path for manufacturing and distribution channels.
- **Regulatory Affairs**. If the product requires FDA/Regulatory approval, then the team needs domain experience to manage the government approval process.
- **Branding, Sales, and Marketing**. These individuals are responsible for developing product branding, the target customer, and market niche.
- **Finance/Accounting**. Good fiscal management will be critical for the success of the company.

Frequently, the team has not clearly carved out their job roles in the early stages of the company. In time, problems arise that cannot be fixed. We have also seen issues over salary and ownership of the company. The expectations and roles have never been discussed but just avoided.

The Company Board

The team leader will have a strong influence on the formation of the company board. The best advice for the founder is to choose their board wisely. They should stay away from group think. A founding board member should have a track record of success with domain expertise, ethical standards, and understanding market challenges. Do not overbuild or underbuild the board. The first board members are usually the initial investor, the CEO, and a domain expert. Once you have the first investor, they can typically help you get more funding. Their network can help you. They have domain (product) experience. They share the CEO's vision. With more funding, the board can add other investors.

Types of Company Boards (Three to Five Members)

Individuals with product and market expertise can round out your board. The best board members will have strong connections to the industry and help with the company exit plan. Maintaining an odd number of board members prevents voting ties.

The *board of directors* should have management and business domain experience. They are paid and are protected with Director and Officers Insurance (D&O insurance). The board has legal responsibility to protect the company and the shareholders. The board sets the annual goals for the CEO. The CEO then sets the goals for the management team. They are paid and must reflect the integrity of the company. The board needs to use their network to help make the company successful. When it is time to sell the company, the CEO will work with the board and their network to get the best exit. From the founder's point of view, the board may have deferred expenses/commitments to the company. The board should have deep connections with the product and market to find the best buyer for the company. This will ensure the best ROI for the team, board, and investors.

The *board observers* are usually investors without voting rights. These individuals are not liable during any company litigation. They can advise the CEO and serve as an observer for other company investors.

The *board of advisors* plays a role between a director and the founder. They have no fiduciary responsibilities and cannot be sued. Their role is solely to advise and help the CEO and they can play a role as an observer for investors. These advisors may not be paid. They have domain experience in the technology and may be friends of the inventor. They advise the CEO and have limited liability to litigation of the company. They serve at the will of the board and CEO and cannot make company decisions.

Management Team Challenges

Team roles can be confusing in the early stages of a company. Trouble can arise over undefined roles of the management team, individuals with multiple roles, or team members not having the same goals. Having a team with different perspectives on issues and customer needs is critical for success. The team may need to pivot if the product does not fit the customer or market or modify the product to fit the target customer or market. We have seen teams struggle with this problem and sometimes it can take down the company. In addition, we have seen the entrepreneur's mother as the chief financial officer of the company. This is not a good idea. Also, husband and wife teams are not usually looked on favorably by investors. We have seen very few successful family teams work out well for the investors. It is also impossible to create a company entirely by yourself and expect to get investor funding.

Investors Evaluation of Teams

The team always wins over the individual interests or the ship sinks.
—Angel Investor Philosophy

Investors would prefer to invest in strong teams with mediocre products rather than mediocre teams with strong products. Your first contact with investors can be through many avenues: investor meetings, panels, incubators, or university research programs. The entrepreneur needs to be able to present their product to an investor in less than two minutes. The "elevator pitch" needs to include the problem you are solving, your solution, your team skills, a growing customer base, how your product is better than the competition, a business model to make money, and an exit plan. You need to practice this presentation repeatedly. This is critical for getting the attention of the investor. Your goal is to get the investor to follow up with questions about you and the product. Investors see or read many, many pitches over the course of their career.

Investor evaluation of the team is around the red flags of their financial plan: the Cap Table, option pool, vesting process (one to five years), issuing of common versus preferred shares, diluted or nondiluted shares, and the type of legal company structure. Investors do not usually invest in crowd-funded companies because of the exposure to litigation.

Success Breeds Success

Investors like to see both a strong team and a board. The founder needs to be able to attract the right people. This will influence investors to mentor and support your company.

Conclusion

If you could get all the people in an organization rowing in the same direction, you could dominate any industry, in any market, against any competition, at any time.

—Patrick Lencioni

Team dynamics and domain experience are more important than the product. As investors, we have found that the most successful products may need to pivot from their initial design or customer needs or target market. Good teams can make this change. Founders that cannot move on from the original product or customer are doomed to failure. The CEO of Theranos, Elizabeth Holmes, has been used as a learning experience for investors. You only need one thought leader to invest in a company to bring in additional investors. The fear of losing out on a great deal will often cause investors to follow the herd. We saw this both with Bernie Madoff and Theranos. Did greed exceed fear? We have learned that the leader is more important for evaluating the company than the word of mouth of peers or emotional evaluations. A strong and good CEO has the following attributes: They embrace change, are a domain expert, focus on finances, use analytics to drive their business strategy, and are agile managers.

Get the right people on the right bus and in the right seat.

—James C. Collins

Reflections on the Issues Addressed in This Section

- Does the company have the right team and board?
- Does the customer know the brand and the team?
- Does the investor want to invest in your team?

CHAPTER 4

The Company

The strong company should first have impeccable integrity. Your reputation is your company's reputation. Your company is known in your network. People do like to gossip; you are in a small community. The management team and board should create a strong company reputation along with having domain expertise in the product, customer, market, and industry. The team should be synergistic, and they can take their concept to market. Investors have found these are the qualities of successful companies.

Conversely, weak companies can have very disruptive members, family members, or friends in the company. Some companies have had difficult former employees or shareholders with significant legal or financial issues.

A Great Company

The founder can start with a simple idea or question and produce a product that can disrupt the market. The company with a great team will have the skills and track record of successful exits. What great companies come to mind for you? There are several well-known examples of good team synergy. Some successful early-stage companies include Amazon, Apple, Google, Oracle, and Yahoo. Complementary skills of the team members allow individual strengths to overcome weaknesses to create a high-functioning team. The novel product must be better than the competition and should be legally protected. The product can be either a technology-driven solution or lifestyle-driven product. The target customer needs to understand the product. The target market should be in a growth phase to make money. The investors should be interested in working with your team. The investors should know that there is an opportunity to get a good ROI. All founders need to know the answers to these simple questions. Hopefully, your company can change the world.

The Entrepreneur's Criteria for a Successful Company

The founder can develop a product that will make the company profitable in a reasonable amount of time. This can be achieved with a knowledgeable team. The product is patented and better than the competition. The customer and market are growing. The business will grow quickly. Investors will get a sizable ROI.

The Customer's Criteria for a Successful Company

You understand the customer's problem and can solve it with your unique solution. The customer can and wants to buy your product. Your company has entered the market with a faster, better, and cheaper product than the competition.

The Investor's Criteria for a Successful Company

For the investor, it always starts with a dynamic and experienced team. The product addresses an important problem with a novel solution. The target customers and market are large and growing. The business plan is reasonable and well thought out. The company has a clearly articulated exit strategy, including how investors will extract significant returns with a sizable return in three to five years. In contrast, the investors want to avoid a CEO with a lifestyle company. If the CEO is too well paid, the investors may not get back their investment.

The Company Name

The company needs a catchy slogan for the customers to remember. The name and logo of the company should be unique and legally protected. The slogan of the company, in three to five words, should capture the essence of the product or company. There are many examples of names, logos, and slogans of successful companies. You will need to achieve this goal to differentiate yourself from the competition. Think of all the great names for companies. A successful company name is critical for branding your product. Naming a company has many challenges; don't rush the process. Think about your audience, make the name easy to spell (shorter is better), factor in search engine optimization, enlist focus groups, don't obsess over a descriptive name, and try to make the name visually distinctive. Using the Internet and focus groups will help narrow your options. You do not need a descriptive name but it should be visually distinct.

The Entrepreneur's Company

The creation of a company is based on insight into the customer's problem and your solution. These are some of the questions an entrepreneur must ask themselves before starting a company.

- What got you interested in the topic?
- Did you find any surprises when creating the solution?
- Do you have any unanswered questions?
- If you had a chance to start over again, what would you do differently?

The people on your team should provide you with different viewpoints of the business. The team with a diverse perspective on business issues has a better chance of success. The company should have domain experience with the product, customer, and market.

The Company From the Customer's Point of View

If the customer is not happy with their current product, then there could be a need for your product. The customer needs to learn the quality of your product through the branding and education by your company. These are some of the challenges for the company to attract customers or establish a beachhead in the market. Does the customer want or need, and can they buy, your product? The product needs to outperform the competition. Is the product differentiated by being either faster, better, or cheaper than the competition? The customer's view of the company's brand name, its logo, and the slogan are important for traction with customers. If the brand can stick with the customer, it can grow the company.

The Company Branding Issues

The company's name needs to be remembered by the customer. Ultimately, the brand will affect the sales of the product and the ability of the company to gain market share. Will the product displace a current competitor in the market? How will you gain market share? The company's name, logo, and slogan are the keys to good branding. Know any products or companies with good branding?

The Company From the Investor's Point of View

Are there any skeletons in the company's closet?

—Angel Investor Philosophy

The investor looks for a company with a dynamic team. The product should address an important problem. Investors prefer to invest money in new disruptive products for growing markets. The product should be legally protected from competitors. The customers and market should be growing. The business model should be well thought out. There is an exit strategy with a good ROI in three to five years. The favorite question investors will ask a CEO is "What keeps you up at night?"

Investor Red Flags

Investors will be concerned with a company that exhibits the following red flags:

- Team member skills do not match their positions.
- The technology needs to be validated by a third party.
- The company branding is not compelling to the customer or investor.

- The customer will need to be educated before they will adopt the new technology.
- Manufacturing and the go-to-market plan is weak or not discussed.
- Business and revenue models could make them cash poor quickly.
- The company deal structure (Cap Table) could lead to future problems.

Financial Issues

Investors do not want to see their financial support go to high salaries or expensive company offices. They are not paying for the CEO's lifestyle. Some companies can have potentially onerous financial agreements or liability issues. Investors have found that some entrepreneurs have signed founder's agreements that are harmful to the company as well as the potential investors. The company should have their records available for financial review with nondisclosure agreements (NDAs) in place to protect the company.

Legal Issues

Investors also check any legal issues about the company. Company agreements are critical for starting the company off on the right foot. The founder's agreements define what belongs to you and what is owned by the other founders. Hiring employees may involve immigration concerns that need to be revised by the company's lawyer, along with any employment agreements or independent contractor agreements. The investor will always ask for the company to have D&O insurance. We have occasionally seen a company dissolved because the CEO became unfit to run it. The company needs liability insurance for different types of business losses, criminal, and regulatory investigations (and their trials). The average fee is around $2 to $5 million depending on the size of the company, revenue, and type of business. The legal entity concerns of the type of company should be for you and the investor. There are several types of entities: LLC/Partnership, C Corporation, B Corporation, or an

S Corporation. Each type has different advantages for investors, taxes, and geographical incorporation. These options for your company will be discussed later.

Conclusion

A great company, like a champion sports team, can overcome adversity, create a healthy team dynamic, and successfully deliver what the customer or fans desire. With so many pitfalls on the journey, it is hard to be successful. If it was easy, everyone would be an entrepreneur.

To overcome these pitfalls, the company and investors look for an ideal CEO with specific characteristics. They can embrace change. They can calmly face the uncertainty of the business climate, mergers and acquisitions (M&A) activity, new competitors entering the market, or regulatory challenges. Embracing and managing to the change allows for continued success. The CEO must be a subject matter expert in their business. They need to understand industry levers, develop strong relationships, and know how to increase value in their given market. They use data to drive strategy. A good CEO will have a "feel" for the business. They will also use metrics to verify and monitor activities to adjust strategy and drive for the right results. They are agile managers. They navigate all situations by building strong teams that work collaboratively and get results. They focus on finances, not just profit and loss, but also on margin, profit, and growth, and use this data to drive business decisions.

Steering the company through these pitfalls requires a variety of strategies to get a product to market and make money for the company and the investor. If it was easy, there would be many more successful companies. A good company has a strong CEO and team.

Reflections on the Issues Addressed in This Section

- Does the company have a good story?
- Does the customer know the company story?
- Does the investor understand your company?

The last three chapters have outlined how to avoid some of the traps for the founder, the management team, and the company. We have evaluated these issues from the point of view of the entrepreneur, customer, and investor.

The next part of the book will focus on the product, legal protections, and the competitors.

PART 2

The Product

Chapter 5. The Problem
The Entrepreneur: Is the problem important?
The Customer: Is the solution worth it?
The Investor: Is the product novel?

Chapter 6. The Product Protection
The Entrepreneur: Are the patents filed/issued?
The Customer: Are there Knockoff protections?
The Investor: What are the legal barriers to entry?

Chapter 7. The Competition
The Entrepreneur: Is the product better than products on the market?
The Customer: Is the product faster, better, and cheaper?
The Investor: Will the product take market share from the competitors?

CHAPTER 5

The Problem

Introduction

You want to deliver a solution to make life easier or healthier. The problem doesn't have to be one that nobody else is tackling; it can just as easily be a problem no one has dealt with effectively. Can you look at the problem differently and offer a unique solution?

We have seen many interesting scientific solutions for business problems. But some of these solutions do not become commercially viable. Basic research can address fundamental questions that may disrupt the commercial status quo of the market. The future of successful products is hard to predict because of the convoluted path to the market. If it was easy to predict winners, then all investors would be very rich.

Conversely, commercially viable products that initially solve a small problem may gain traction and obtain significant market share. Can you think of any of these products?

The Product Properties

The solution is an important answer to a problem many people want solved. To help sell the product to the customer, branding the product with a novel name, logo, and slogan will help educate the consumer. The invention can have a unique or novel design. The customer can have confidence in the product when it is validated by third-party testing. The early adopters should be the target consumers for your product.

The Product Evaluation

The product should be a novel solution to a problem. The prototype should be a minimum viable product (MVP). It should fulfill the needs of the customer. The niche market should be growing and not static. The product should be legally protected from the competition. The decision to manufacture and distribute has been determined to be internally or by outsourcing the process. The product should make money in a growing customer base. The right team is available to make the company successful. The branding of the product should have special features, unique packaging, and a selling strategy.

The Product Is Protected

The concept has been reduced to practice. The invention is an MVP. There are strong legal barriers, patents, trademarks, trade secrets, or copyrights put in place to protect your invention. These protections can block competitors from entering the market.

The Entrepreneur

Do your own research to validate the problem and your solution.
—Angel Investor Philosophy

The entrepreneur should ask if the problem is of sufficient importance to solve. Customers may not think they have a big problem, and the investors may not think the problem is worth their investment. Some problems are interesting, but the solutions will never make enough money. The lack of customers, the small market, or strong competing products are limitations to the success of novel products. Entrepreneurs should look to solve game-changing problems.

The solution for the entrepreneur should be a total solution to the problem. Will the customer understand your solution? The investment community needs a novel protected solution to the problem. They do not want a vitamin pill solution. The solution can be defined as either a "first-of-a-kind" new idea or a "need-to-have" product. The product needs to be validated by a third party. The founder needs to demonstrate a clear path to commercialization. The product should be a solution for a specific group of customers. A survey should identify the needs of the target customer. The major sales focus should be for that customer/niche market.

If the product does not satisfy the customer or market needs, the company needs to pivot the product to a different customer, market, or industry. This pivot has happened more times than you can imagine.

Most investors want a working prototype or validated product before funding the company. They are not interested in funding research projects. The product's stage of development is also critical for getting investors interested in your company. The product must satisfy the customers and other independent groups. The product must have a significant improvement or cost reduction on the other competitive products. If the product can solve other problems, then additional revenue streams can be generated.

The Customer

Will the dog eat the dog food?

—Elton White

The entrepreneur needs to know if the customer's problem is compelling enough to make the customer change their buying habits. Is the customer aware of the problem that the entrepreneur has identified? The barriers to entry or adoption issues of your product can be challenging. How many prospective buyers have this problem that can be validated by a survey? What is your unique selling proposition to the customer? The problem for the customer should be evident from your surveys. The investor is looking for a product with a large market. Is your solution a compelling reason for the buyers to do something about the problem? Does the customer understand the magnitude of the problem and your solution? Can the customers pay for your product? Has your product been validated by a third party and do you have a quality solution? The customer is interested in unique products that have important benefits. Any significant improvement or cost reduction over the competition is also helpful. The customer also looks to see if the product can solve their problems or other use issues. Most customers want to buy an MVP. The customer will ask if there is enough differentiation between your product and the competition. Your product should offer a value proposition for the customer. Will the customer leave their current product? Does the customer need your product? A customer survey will help answer if they want the product, can buy the product, and will establish a beachhead market. The customer needs to connect to the branding of the product. A customer survey helps validate the customer hypothesis by age, gender, education, and income. A good brand will connect with the customer and give a good first impression. Capturing the customer's attention will build the buzz around the product name and the logo. The design of the product and packaging needs to fit the target customer. The brand name, company, or CEO needs to be memorable for the customer. Ultimately, the branding will affect the sales of the product.

The investor is interested in the market and industry trends which might change the customers' problem or your solution. Sometimes the solution is better than the current product, but the market is declining, or other competitors have better ideas. In addition, an outdated brand may affect the ability of the company to gain market share or customer retention.

The Investor

If the entrepreneur cannot explain the product without giving away the secret sauce, most investors will not move on to the next entrepreneur.
—Angel Investor Philosophy

One of the first questions an investor will ask you is to explain the significance of the problem and why your solution is faster, better, or cheaper than the competition. The product needs to be protected. The entrepreneur needs to explain the product without giving away the secret sauce. Investors usually do not sign NDAs. The investor needs to understand the product and your intellectual property (IP) position without disclosing confidential information. The first set of questions by the investors will cover whether the product is a total and unique technology solution. The second set of questions will ask if there is an MVP and has product development been completed.

For the investor, it is important that the product has been validated. Investors will require verifiable results before investing. The investor is also interested in whether the product can solve other problems and whether it has multiple revenue sources. The investor analysis of the product will be defined by the industry segment and its rate of growth. The business model on how you are going to make money will be clarified. Industry life cycles, distribution channels, any adoption issues of the product, and any barriers to entering the market will be evaluated. Investors may or may not have an appetite for your market. The investor will do a deeper dive into your product with a strengths, weaknesses, opportunities, and threats (SWOT) analysis. The company may use outsourcing to make their product. If so, will they produce the quality product on time and with the amount required to sell to the customers? The competition in the segments will be defined. It is important that competitors cannot work around the product solution. The product should be protected from other alternate solutions.

The investment group will evaluate the product's legal issues. Legally protecting the concept is critical for funding by investors. The investors will ask the entrepreneur to define the novelty of the product and whether it has been reduced to practice. The concept needs to be reduced to practice for a patent. The investor will want to know how the product is protected: Is it defined as IP, trademarked, or copyrighted, or is it a trade secret? They need to know if there are barriers to entry for your product. They must be clearly defined. The patent attorney for the investors will do a search for any competing IP or alternative technology. Most investors will not sign NDAs. Investors have a reputation to protect; it is their most important asset. They will not discuss your novel product to noninvestors. The investors look to see who legally represents the company and products. The investment communities will also have several attorneys that can make their legal opinions known to the members. It is important to get a well-respected legal counsel that is known to the investors.

Most universities sign an employment agreement with employees on hiring. The university claims all inventions produced by the employee. If an invention is created at the university, there will be an invention disclosure. The employee can license their technology from the university for a reasonable license term. They can even start a company with their technology. These patents are protectable barriers to block entry of competitors into the field from any competing or alternative technology. If there are people interested in a technology, the inventor can protect themselves with an NDA. This is a legally binding contract between outside parties or an employer/employee. It helps protect the patent rights and trade secrets but only by what is described in the agreement. In my experience, an investment group reviews 40 to 80 proposals each month, and we screen six to eight companies per month. We could not sign NDAs for each one of these proposals.

The investor will need to know if the product will solve other problems and have multiple revenue sources. This will allow the product to have maximum revenue and optimal growth projections. This protects the investor from delays in the goals, milestones, and timelines if one of the products gets delayed or fails. Most investors want game-changing technology, not just an add-on or slight improvement. Ideally, the product may be applicable to more than one market.

Conclusion

Your research on the problem should validate your solution. Your product should satisfy the needs of your customer. The product should be protected from the competition. The investor should understand the customer and the market should give them a strong ROI. The entrepreneur and investor should agree on the alignment of product, customer, and market to be successful.

Reflections on the Issues Addressed in This Section

- Will the product make people's lives safer or more comfortable?
- Will the customer buy your solution?
- Will the investor know the product, customer, and market?

CHAPTER 6

The Product Protection

Introduction

The patenting of academic scientific research in England and Germany before World War II was different. The academic cultures in these countries had different opinions about patentable university research. In Germany, it was common for scientists to patent their research and receive financial benefits from their discoveries; it was not the same in England. After 1932, many German scientists immigrated. Some went especially to England to continue their scientific research. This cultural conflict between educated scientists trained in Europe and England continued after the war. Many scientists fled Europe to the United States to continue their work because of the strong U.S. government financial support of their medical research.

Most American faculty did not patent their research discoveries until the mid-1980s. This changed with the cloning of the insulin gene and Genentech's commercialization of a biological product. By the 1980s, Congress passed the Bayh-Dole Act. This legislation helped commercialize by-products of federally funded medical research. There is reluctance among U.S. faculty to patent their research, even today. To date, less than 5 percent of federally funded research is developed into products. Even with this small number, these patents generate new ventures. Working with a university's IP office can help protect the entrepreneur and their investors when starting new ventures.

The Protection of the Product

IP is a creation of the mind, an invention, that is used in commerce. It is a legal protection of your idea. The government license confers the right for a period to exclude others from making, using, or selling your invention. In return for this monopoly, it must be useful and not oblivious. The types of patents are utility, design, and new plant species.

The product concept needs to be reduced to practice. This is the first rule of patenting your idea. The patent is good for approximately 20 years from the first disclosure. There is always time to improve your product with additional patent filings. They are called continuation-in-part (CIP). There are other types of legal protection including trademarks, trade secrets, and copyrights. These can form a strong legal barrier to market entry by your competitors. Conversely, can your startup company afford a lengthy litigation process? The good news is sometimes your competitor becomes your acquirer. Sometimes, it is not worth the legal fight, and it is cheaper to just buy you out.

The Types of Attorneys

There are several types of legal representation that are necessary as a company matures. There is currently a new attorney category, emerging enterprise attorney. They specialize in early-stage financially challenged startup companies. A corporate attorney is essential for creating a legal structure for the organization and tax planning. A patent attorney is necessary to protect your ideas, products, copyrights, trademarks, and the company name. A personal attorney protects your rights with the company. When you are ready to sell the company, a business attorney specializes in the mergers and acquisitions process. I used four different attorneys when my company Melanoma Diagnostics was sold to Myriad Generics.

The Role of Legal Counsel

You want to hire an attorney to be your guide and advocate on any legal issues for your company and for yourself. Their role is to understand the law and protect the company and the individual. You want to interview the right attorney for you and a separate one for your company. The fit is critical between you and your legal counsel. They need to be skilled in the arts of listening, negotiation, and interpretation of the law, and act as a fair agent for their client. The cost of the attorney fees is worth it in the long run for both you and the company.

The Types of Legal Protection

It is essential for an entrepreneur to protect their ideas, concepts, prototypes, and products. The IP of the company is the value to the investor. Investors fund companies with strong legal protection of their portfolio of products. The protection can come in many ways: filed or issued patents (IP), trademark, copyright, and trade secrets. Trademark protects the brand. Copyright protects the original works of expression.

Trade secrets protect secret ideas or information. There are utility and design patents that protect inventions and product designs. The types of patents include provisional, U.S.-issued, and overseas-issued patents.

To file a U.S. patent, it must be a unique (novel) insight into a problem. The concept must be reduced to practice and validated. The patent applications can then be filed at the Patent Office in Washington, DC. The process to issue a patent can take months to years. Getting a patent depends on several important criteria: The claims are not obvious, there are no competing patents or there is no alternative technology, and the claims have the earliest filing date. A product can also be legally secured by filing a trademark, copyright, or a trade secret. We will discuss patents in more detail in the legal issues for startup companies in a later chapter.

Legally Protecting the Entrepreneur

The most common legal document to protect an entrepreneur is the nondisclosure agreement (NDA). This is a legal contract that signifies a confidential relationship exists between the parties involved with your company. The NDA will refer to information shared between the parties, but it can only protect information that is expressly defined in the document. The NDA can be for a mutual agreement between companies (M&A) or unilateral between the employer and the employee. The scope and purpose of the NDA is defined to the specific disclosure of the information to be revealed. The NDA prevents the information shared from being disclosed to any third party. There can be no use of this information for other purposes which are not set forth in the NDA. The term limits of an NDA can be from one to five years; sometimes they may try to make them last longer. The most novel technology becomes obsolete in 12 to 24 months (i.e., medical devices). Reasonable NDAs are for around 18 months. Most investors will not sign an NDA because it is not practical, given the number of companies they review weekly. The entrepreneur should be able to describe their technology without disclosing confidential information.

Directors and officers insurance (D&O) covers breach of duty, regulatory investigations, and trials for the company. It can also protect against litigation by team members, board members, shareholders, customers, or the government. The policy cost and deductibles vary. The cost of the policy can depend on the size of the company, revenue, coverage amount, type of business, and private versus public. Early-stage companies can get several million dollars in coverage for less than $10,000 per year. The death of a member of the management team is usually covered by life insurance. We have experienced the death of a CEO in one of our portfolio companies. Unfortunately, the company went bankrupt.

The Entrepreneur

Your patents are the legal protection of your technology. They are protectable barriers to keep out your competitors. Patents are essential for gaining the interest of investors. If a company can create a broad patent portfolio, it will keep competitors at bay. If you want your company acquired, having a strong patent position is the quickest way to gain an exit by an acquirer or a competitor. Unfortunately, interested corporate investors or individual investors can be collecting information on your product for a competing company with similar technology. Your attorney can draw up an NDA to sign before you discuss your technology with individuals or companies. Sometimes companies will not sign NDAs but promise to do a deal after they see the data. I have had that experience; a large diagnostic company saw our data, but then did not do the deal with us. Lesson learned; the entrepreneur needs to protect their product from the competition.

You will also want to understand the economics of any licenses. And finally, depending on the situation, you may need to do some work to make sure the company has freedom to operate relative to other patents belonging to third parties.

The founder may also need legal advice on their company agreements with shareholders and employees. The shareholder agreements define their voting rights and when they can legally buy and sell their shares. The employees' agreements may require visa documents, intern jobs, noncompensation agreements, equity positions, and licensing in outside technology to the company. Attorneys can keep the company running smoothly and out of harm's way.

Your attorney can review any exclusive or restrictive contracts. Early-stage companies sometimes do silly things to secure a first contract or garner early bootstrap revenue. These contracts can contain provisions that grant third parties exclusive rights with respect to technology, divest from the company rights around a particular field of use, and limit the territory in which a company can compete, among other things. Any contracts that limit a company from realizing its business plan or that sacrifice long-term potential for short-term viability need to be considered when evaluating the overall investment opportunity.

Your attorney can document your capitalization structure and company history. Understanding of the Cap Table, including prior financings, the vesting around existing employee equity, and some of the history behind the issuance of stock to nonfounders is important. A Cap Table can provide a strong record of prior financing, potential issues with legacy founders, and the current incentive structure for existing employees and founders. Looking beyond the Cap Table can also reveal those parties that may have other claims relative to the company's stock (such as informal/contractual antidilution rights) that can be disruptive to financing.

The Customer

The customer wants the best value for their products. Are they willing to buy your product? Legally protected products prevent knockoffs most of the time. But the consumer should be aware of fake or rip-off items. A legally protected brand, name, and logo are the best protection for the customer.

The Investor

If the company cannot explain the product (no NDA) without giving away the secret sauce, then most investors will move on to the next company. An investor will look to see if the legally protected technology is disruptive to the market. The technology needs to be filed for a patent but if the patented is issued, the investor is more interested in the company. There are always some competing patents or alternative technology. This is always the big risk for the investor. Additionally, if there are significant cost improvements necessary for the product to get into the market, then the investor needs to reevaluate going forward with the company.

The value of a product is proportional to the strength of the patents. The Cetus Polymerase Chain Reaction (PCR) Assay Patent was sold to DuPont in the 1990s. The legal rights of the PCR patent became more valuable after DuPont won their court challenge. Anyone that wanted to use the PCR assay academically or commercially had to license the technology from DuPont for the next 20 years. The ribozyme technology was never commercially exploited because a short scientific abstract was published from a Japanese scientific meeting in 1990. There was no legal protection for developing anti-oncogenes ribozymes for the treatment of cancer by gene therapy.

Conclusion

Most early-stage companies concentrate patents in four main areas: assets, due diligence, contracts, and employee agreements. The legal issues for a startup company can be overwhelming. It is necessary to have good legal counsel at all stages of the company's growth and exit. The entrepreneur needs independently verifiable results of the product at different stages of development. The customer depends on the legally protected product and brand. An investor funds a new venture with protected disruptive technology. If the patent can solve different business problems, the patent becomes an asset for the company and investor. The patent portfolio is a legal barrier for the competitors. If the company goes bankrupt, the assets (patents) can be sold to recover some of the investments.

Reflections on the Issues Addressed in This Section

- Does the company have a protected product?
- Does the customer want to buy your product?
- Does the investor want to invest in your protected product?

CHAPTER 7

The Competition

There is always competition, perceived or not, or alternative solutions.
—Angel Investor Philosophy

Introduction

Your protected product needs to be differentiated from the competition. The biggest red flag to an investor is "There is no competition." If an investor hears those words, it is unlikely the entrepreneur will get funded. Remember, the CEO is presenting in front of 50 to 100 investors with domain expertise, a strong network of business associates, and 10 to 50 years of business experience.

I have never been in an investor screening where the investors did not know the product, customer, and market. They always know the competitive products, past and present products, and perceived or not perceived or alternative solutions. Investors pool their knowledge and business experience before investing.

Differentiation From the Competition

The simplest question is whether your product is faster, better, or cheaper than the competition. Investors will want to know whether it is legally protected and whether or not the product can be reverse engineered. The competition will be kept out of the market by strong barriers. Customers should not have any adoption issues of your product over the competition.

The Entrepreneur

The general industry rule is if you are going to compete in the market, then you need to be faster, better, or cheaper than the competition.

To gain market share for your product, a differentiation factor is required to overcome adoption issues and barriers to entry. The entrepreneur must define the primary advantage of their product over their competition. The product needs to be disruptive to the competition and can maintain a sustainable competitive advantage in the future. There are always alternate solutions to your product, now or in the future. It is important that your product does not get out-modeled by the next competitor. This happens frequently in the medical device industry, where the product life cycle can be as short as 6 to 18 months. Not only can direct competition kill your product but simply getting your product to market can limit your sales cycle. The product supplier and their distribution channels can also make or break market penetration.

The entrepreneur needs to establish a market beachhead quickly to differentiate their product. They need to offer a value proposition to the customer, offer competitive pricing, create unique branding, and provide an easy distribution model, ease of sale, and a marketing plan.

The Customer

There should be a compelling interest by the consumer to buy your product. The target customer needs can be defined by a customer survey. The buyer's characteristics can be defined by their gender, age, income, geographical location, lifestyle, likes and dislikes, and a compelling need for your product. The question the entrepreneur needs to ask is if the customer is content with their current product. The customer wants to know the benefits of your solution. The customer needs to have a sufficient importance tied to the product. Understanding the number of buyers and their ability to pay will define the benefits of your product. These benefits include verifiable results, significant improvement, or cost reductions. Branding is critical to connecting to the customer with your logo, imagery, name, and social media for making a successful consumer product that can be discriminated from competitors.

Branding and design are critical for attracting new customers. The right design can overcome some weaknesses of the product. Good branding can help you distance the competitors. The company name, logo, and slogan can also create a loyal base of customers. One well-known advertising company's rule is "Keep the branding simple and keep it tangible."

The Investor

The investor can have 10 to 50 years of experience in your product and market. In addition, they have a network that understands industry trends and knows if your business model will work with your product and customer, and they know your competitors.

Investors know that most products have competitors by cost, quality, or speed. The company name (logo) and product's name (slogan) need to capture the customer's attention. One concern investors have is that products can become outdated prematurely or that there are alternate solutions to your product now or in the future. It is essential that the entrepreneur can clearly communicate the primary advantage of your product over the competition and how it is disruptive to the market. The product's differentiation criteria should be that it is significantly faster, better, or cheaper. The product should have a legally protected and sustainable competitive advantage.

New products have barriers to entry into the market or adoption issues early in the sales cycle. For the customer to adopt the product, there must be a clear focus on an initial need; the early adopters need to sustain a business to grow the market. The customers must be retained and satisfied by the product. The supply of products must be maintained through suppliers and distribution channels. The investors need traction in the customer market that enables them a 10× return in three to seven years. For the investor, medical products have one simple question: "Is there an unmet medical need for the product?"

Diagram for Displaying Competition

Figure 7.1 is a map of the competition. The diagram needs quantification with the number of customers or products sold or sales figures on the x- and y-axes. The competitive companies can be shown with spheres proportional to their market share.

Figure 7.1 Competition diagram

Conclusion

Competition will always be a threat to your product. Modifications of the product can keep you at the head of the market. The entrepreneur needs to keep their product improvements protected by patent filings.

A customer needs to understand that your product is better than what is on the market. The value proposition will create a loyal buyer that will sustain your customer growth.

An investor will want to know that your product is better than the competition, is a legally protected product, and will get a good ROI quickly from the market.

Reflections on the Issues Addressed in This Section

- Does the company have a protected product?
- Does the educated customer want to buy your product?
- Does the investor want to invest in your protected product?

PART 3

The Business Strategy

Chapter 8. The Business Plan
The Entrepreneur: The business plan for the customer and market.
The Customer: Is your product better than the competition?
The Investor: When will I get my return on investment (ROI)?

Chapter 9. The Customer
The Entrepreneur: What is the value proposition for the customer?
The Customer: Does the customer survey support your customer hypothesis?
The Investor: Beachhead strategy to acquire and retain the customers.

Chapter 10. The Market
The Entrepreneur: Business strategy for product differentiation.
The Customer: The product buzz, acquire and retain customers.
The Investor: Barriers to enter the market, market size and growth, and industry trends.

Always have time to think.

—Professor V. Canalakus,
Yale Medical School

CHAPTER 8

The Business Plan

Introduction

For the entrepreneur, the solution to a big problem is a valuable product for the customer. Your customer interviews should validate the customer needs for your product. Your product needs to be better than the competition. For the investor, can your company make money with your product in a growing market? The entrepreneur should outline their business strategy before setting out on their adventure. Doing your research on the product, customer, and market will prevent time-consuming delays and dead ends.

The Business

A quick outline is below with the questions that need to be addressed before launching your venture. This is the framework that will lead to your business plan. A document that can outline your key business issues and the business plan will help clarify your thoughts for those interested in your company. The document should be short and clear.

A business plan should outline your thoughts with a clear path from concept to market. The purpose of the plan is to introduce your ideas, financial goals, and timelines for your company. Investors need to know who you are and what your company does. The investor will get an insight into your company with a business plan. This plan can be used as sales document for raising capital.

The business plan is a document that can be easily read by your team and investors; it should communicate a rational plan to get your product to market. Investors usually review your executive summary and PowerPoint presentation first before they do a deep dive into your company.

This document helps you get face-to-face meetings with investors. If an investor is interested in your company, they will review your business plan and quickly focus on the summary, the team, and the financials. These items will reveal a lot about the maturity of the team and company. The downside of the business plan is that as soon as it is finished, it is outdated. It will require timely revisions with new directions or changes in the business model.

The executive summary should focus on the market opportunity, the novelty of the product, and the experience of the team. It should explain the need for and the use of funds to achieve milestones and goals. It should explain product protection. It should detail how the product solves a unique problem and how it is better than the competition. The business model should have a revenue plan, with defined costs/margins. The go-to-market plan should explain market penetration with a sales and market analysis with a customer profile. The partnerships (internal or outsourced) for manufacturing and distribution of product should demonstrate business contracts and agreements in place. Financial projections, goals, and milestones with funding needs should be realistic for two to three years. The team, board, and the company should have domain experience and understand the product, customer, and the market. An exit strategy should be explored in the business plan with the potential risks and potential ROI for the investors noted within a realistic time frame.

The Entrepreneur

The business plan will validate the entrepreneur's hypothesis of the value proposition of their new product. The customer survey data will support the product benefits and advantages over competitors. The company name, logo, and slogan will clearly define the product.

The Customer

The customer survey should define the needs of the customer for your product. The survey can characterize the target customer and whether they can buy the product. The customer needs to understand that your product solves their problem better than the competing products in the market.

The Investor

The entrepreneur should be prepared to make a short pitch (less than two minutes) about their company and product. If the investor is interested in you or the product, they will ask for a one-page summary of the company and your investor presentation. This information can easily be evaluated by the investor and will help them understand the strengths and weaknesses of the company. If the company had all the answers and could fast-track their product to market, there would be no need for investors. Therefore, investors can play a vital role in the company's growth and maturity.

Syndication deals with other angel groups and venture capital groups help build a safety net for early-stage companies. This was critical for the investment community and their portfolio of companies in 2008 when the market crashed. We spent the next year trying to keep our early-stage companies afloat until the economy recovered. The Pasadena Angels were able to save most of our portfolio companies but we had limited opportunities to fund new ventures for the next 18 to 24 months.

Investors always need a backup plan for when the company runs out of money. Bridge funding can sometimes be arranged to carry companies through their initial startup challenges. Note that some investors never do follow-on funding once they invest in your company.

> *It always takes twice as much time and twice as much money to achieve the entrepreneur's goals and milestones.*
>
> —Angel Investor Philosophy

The Company Pitch and Investor Presentation

In order to get funded, it is essential to be able to communicate your vision of the company to an investor. Investors see many pitches, and your first impression will make a lasting impression on them. You need to make your story interesting but keep it simple. Your honesty, personality, and intellect will be on display. And finally, be truthful and be aware of the company's weaknesses and your solutions. You have an opportunity to demonstrate your clarity of thought. You will see if you are a good fit with the investor. Conversely, are the investor and their domain expertise a good fit for you and your company? If not, there are always many other investors.

The pitch should include the problem, your solution, the product, the competition, your target customer survey results, the niche market, the business model, the team, and an executive summary. You will need to do this in about two minutes and it will require a lot of practice to make a polished and thorough presentation.

If you are lucky, your pitch will lead to more questions from the investor—a request for your presentation and your executive summary. If all goes well, they may ask for you to present to their investor group.

Listen to the questions about your company and product from the investor. Their questions reflect their education, work experience, and investment knowledge. You are looking for the right fit between you and the investor's network. All investors are not the same or have the same life experiences. If they say things like "Help me understand …," then they are interested in both you and the company.

Good luck!

The Business Plan

If the screening goes well with the investors after the presentation, they may ask for the company's business plan. Some of the lead investors may read your document. The thought leaders and domain experts will review these documents. Your plan will give the investor an insight in understanding your thinking, your business strategy, and whether you understand the challenges you will face in bringing your concept to market. However, most investors will only read the executive summary. Can you imagine about 100 SEC accredited investors reading every company's business plan each month? That would be in the range of 10 to 25 plans a month!

A good business plan will be 15 to 25 pages, including appendixes. The plan will include the product, customer/market surveys, go-to-market strategy, business model, financials, the team, and the exit plan. The appendices should include financial projections, validations, protection of your product, and data from your product surveys. Remember, your plans are ever evolving.

Conclusion

The business plan becomes outdated the second you finish the document. The good news is that the investor can read the plan and get an understanding of your domain experience, business model, financial requirements, and exit strategy. This document is valuable for the founder and can be continually revised. Unfortunately, few investors spend enough time reading the business plan. They evaluate products by reading the executive summary, listening to the investor presentation, and speaking with the entrepreneur.

Reflections on the Issues Addressed in This Section

- Does the company have a pitch for their business plan?
- Does the customer survey say that they want to buy your product?
- Does the investor want to invest in your business plan?

CHAPTER 9

The Customer

Introduction

People need to want your product and service. Other people (customers) need to be as excited about your idea as you are. Start testing the idea and talking about it with friends and family members, and survey potential customers. Identifying the target customer with the right product is the home run. The challenge of achieving this success depends on the adoption of the product by the customer. The CEO may think that their product smells good, looks good, and tastes good but the customer may not buy it. There must be a compelling value proposition for the customer to try your product and then leave their current product.

The Entrepreneur

Your innovator, the early adopter, must see the value proposition in the product, its quality, price, reliability, and their experience. The second stage is that the customers must validate the product by buying it. If the customer is satisfied with your product over the current options, then you have a chance of retaining them. The customer will realize that they need it. The brand name of the product creates the buzz and connects the customer. This creates a niche customer market for your solution, design, and branding. The customer survey can validate the product and target customer. The purpose of the customer survey is to see if your product will make a difference in their lifestyle and if your product differentiates itself to the customer through the company name and logo for a good first impression.

The Customer

Can you quantify the problem in time and money?
—Angel Investor Philosophy

Your early adopters should give you good traction for the first business sales and overcoming the barriers to entry. Your product needs to differentiate itself to the customers. There will be a need to characterize customer segments (size and niche) by customer surveys. Your brand name needs to stand out and be remembered by the customer. The customer survey should be the initial test of your product. Your network of family and friends should help you refine the survey questions.

The Customer Pyramid Survey

A short survey (approximately 5 questions in 10 minutes) is best to start with in the first trial. If the survey can be done face to face, then the responses tend to be more accurate than phone interviews and web questions. It is always good to have a partner listening to the questions. This way you can compare notes and make sure that what the customer said is what you both recorded. The next method to enhance your survey is to ask for three more contacts in their network after each interview. This can create a pyramid structure that creates a cascade of customers from a network of friends.

The customer survey should validate your product/customer hypothesis. If it does not, you need to pivot your product, target customer, or market niche to accommodate the needs of the customer. You will need to define the customer by gender, age, education, income level, and geographical region (local, national, or international).

The Customer Surveys

The first round of questions should address the following:

1. How satisfied are you with the quality of your current products?
2. What is your greatest source of dissatisfaction?
3. What differentiates your product from the competitors?

4. Where do you buy products?
5. What features do you like on the product?

If you are engaged with the customer, start the second round of questions by keeping your conversation open ended:

1. How do they see the problem?
2. What is their current product?
3. Where do you buy your product?
4. What is your ideal solution?
5. Are there any barriers to buying the new product?

If you are still engaged with the customer, the third round should address the following questions:

1. How do you define the problem?
2. What is good about that distribution channel?
3. What is good about this market?
4. What are your workarounds?
5. Who is responsible for the buying decision: you or someone else?

Sometimes the customer will continue talking about their product experience, both good and bad. The fourth round of questions should probe deeper.

1. Who are your key influencers?
2. How much do you spend on products during each month and each year?
3. What would be the ideal solution?
4. What fears would you have in trying this solution?
5. Do you need to see a well-established brand name?

A significant survey will have between 50 and 150 customer interviews. The more surveys you do, the more focused the data. The survey's goal is to find the true customer needs. The survey should help with customer acquisition and retention by defining the sales cycle funnel, the cost to acquire a customer, the life cycle integration, sales, service, and follow-on products for the target customer.

The Investor

The investors look for the beachhead strategy for getting the product to the early adopters. Market penetration of 1 to 3 percent with customers buying your product lowers both the anxiety of the investor and the risk of their investment. If there is a behavior change required for the customer to buy the product, this will slow market penetration.

The investor needs to understand the novelty of the product. Showing how the product differentiates itself from the competition is important for getting funded by investors. The value proposition is a key metric for investor funding. Defining product benefits, features, and customer experience gives confidence to the investor to work with the company.

The company name, logo, and slogan can help make sales, connect with the customer, and create buzz for the product. On the risk side for the investors, there is no compelling value proposition, high barriers to entry into the market, and there is a long sales cycle. Government and health care institutions are notorious for long sales cycles.

Conclusion

The entrepreneur needs to do his research on the customer both for themselves and for the investor. The product needs traction with the customer. This will validate the customer research survey. Customer traction encourages investors to take the company seriously and make an investment.

Reflections on the Issues Addressed in This Section

- Does the company have the right product for their target customer?
- Does the target customer want to buy your product?
- Does the investor want to invest in your business?
- Are customers buying your product?

CHAPTER 10

The Market

Introduction

We have seen that the solution to a problem is critical for a new venture and customers need to be excited about the product. But another issue to solve for your product is its scalability. You need to expand your idea, expand your product pipeline, and monetize your product fast. The market should allow your business to grow. Your total addressable market (TAM) should be in a growth phase.

The Entrepreneur

You must have a clear product strategy for the target customer and target market. The target customer must understand the value proposition and the product differentiation. You will need to identify the early adopters that will enter your market.

The Investor

They will need to identify the beachhead strategy, the product buzz, and the method to acquire and retain the customers. The product solution should solve a major problem for a large addressable market. There could be a demand for this product for a large and growing number of customers. Market opportunities and multiple revenue streams will drive the investors to your company. But the team needs domain experience with the product, customer, and market. The customer is part of the growing market that can buy your new product and the investor can make money in an emerging market. We have seen some great ideas in the investment community, but the products were in a niche market with not enough customers. Unless the product can pivot to a new customer or market, the ROI for the investor will be too low to generate enough interest in funding the company. Identify the real customer problem that has a large and growing market.

Market Segmentation

Understanding the total market from the surveys is critical for a product launch to be successful. The TAM is very different from the total market and easily confused by entrepreneurs when presenting to investors. The investors' and entrepreneurs' knowledge of the market trends will be critical for the product's success. The customer needs, behavior, and education about the product will also be critical for success. There will be different business strategies to establish the product into a market niche versus an emerging niche market. If the market has innovative customers, identifying this market segment is critical for the traction of the product. The evaluation of the industry ecosystem, including stakeholders and partners, will be important for market penetration.

The general rule for market segmentation is keep it simple.

Market Traps

- Is the market stable or declining?
- Is the target market too small?
- Will new product technology change the market?

Target Market

The target industry and the market segment should be defined by your survey data and domain experts (investors). The industry life cycle for the products will be defined; the competitors in this market segment and the niche market growth will be known by the investors. Do the investors have the appetite for this product and your market segment?

Sales and Marketing

These people are critical for scaling the product in the right market. The company needs them to communicate well to the customer and the organization. Scaling the product for growing the market share is important to the company to obtain higher revenue and profits.

The Entrepreneur

If the entrepreneur is to be successful, it is important to understand the market trends for their product and appreciate the changing industry trends. This will require primary and secondary research on the industry and markets. We live in a very technologically disruptive society and it can be almost impossible to predict future market trends. What we need and what we want can be invented in days and put on the market in weeks depending on the product and the customer's needs. These cycles have been condensed from decades to years to financial quarters. Market strategy, as you can imagine, is full of the wrong bets or just misguided business choices.

A strong target market with a large addressable and growing customer base gives confidence to both the entrepreneur and their investors for their product. The total addressable market (TAM) should have a clear demand for the product with an ability to positively disrupt the status quo of the competitors. This will demonstrate a clear advantage to the customer as well as the investor.

An entrepreneur will face significant challenges when bringing a product to market if the customer needs education or behavioral changes to buy the product. The product will need to be obviously better than the competitors, but the customers could be entrenched. This could cause an adoption issue. The market penetration can also depend on the length of the sales cycle and the customer's time for evaluation to buying the product. Product offerings can excite customers and investors at the same time. Your product needs to differentiate itself to a very competitive market.

The Customer

Do the customers want your product? The target customer for your market needs to be researched and shown to have a growing need for your product. For example, an aging population is in need of specialized medical equipment. This can include personalized diagnostics and therapeutics, medical devices, and equipment for hospitals and in-home care. This is a growing market and industry for the right product. Artificial intelligence is one of the big movers in the health care space but the right product for the right patient has still been elusive. The digital monitoring of personal biometrics is one of these hot products.

The Investor

Is the market big enough to give me a good ROI?
—Angel Investor Philosophy

The investor is always looking for trends in markets and specific industries. They are constantly reviewing proposals that reflect new product developments. Investors understand the needs of growing markets and the niche novel products can create with customer needs and target markets. There are market traps for the investor. Investors also have a feel for declining or unstable markets and the need to stay out of them.

Another market trap is products that are low cost with low margins. It is difficult for the investor to get a good ROI in the short term. If the target market size is too small, it will not enable venture-level returns to the investors. Finally, if the product cannot differentiate itself from the competitor or new product technology, there will never be deep penetration into the target market.

Conclusion

The entrepreneur's ability to identify the target market is critical for the success of the company. The product may need to pivot several times before it is successful. Which competitors will lose market share?

Does the customer have adoption issues or need to be educated about the product to gain market share? The target customer will validate the product by growing the target market.

The investor looks for a product in a growing market with a large customer base. To obtain a good ROI, disruptive technology products should dominate the market and be immune to different products gaining market dominance or taking the market in a different direction.

Reflections on the Issues Addressed in This Section

- Does the company have a pitch for their business plan?
- Does your survey show that the customer will buy your product?
- Does the investor know your product is in a growing market?

Plans to Make More Revenue

- Can you expand on your idea?
- Can you make the product more flexible?
- Can the product be more resilient or remodeled?
- Can you monetize the product better?

PART 4

The Business Model

The investor will need to know if the product will solve other problems and have multiple revenue sources. This will allow the product to have a maximum revenue projection and optimal growth projections. This protects the investor from delays in the goals, milestones, and timelines if one of the products gets delayed or fails.

Chapter 11. The Business Model

How do you make money on your product?
—Angel Investor Philosophy

The Entrepreneur: Value proposition and product differentiation.
The Customer: The product buzz, by acquiring and retaining customers.
The Investor: Barriers to enter the market, sales cycle, and industry trends.

Chapter 12. The Go-to-Market Plan

How are you going to get your product to the customer?
—Angel Investor Philosophy

The Entrepreneur: Branding, manufacturing, and distribution.
The Customer: Where can they buy your product?
The Investor: What is the distribution and market strategy?

Chapter 13. The Financial Plan

Cash is king.
—Angel Investor Philosophy

The Entrepreneur: What is the breakeven and profit profile?
The Customer: What is the customer retention for the product pricing?
The Investor: When will I get a timely ROI with your revenue stream?

CHAPTER 11

The Business Model

Introduction

In Boston, I reviewed many applications submitted to the investment community. Boston is a mecca for first-class biomedical research. The science I reviewed has been outstanding, but the applications often read like requests for a government grant; there was no discussion of competition, no business model, and no go-to-market plan. Investors like to know how you are going to make money. You make money with your business model, including value proposition, cost structure, revenue streams, and target customers.

The business model should give you a clear path to profitability in less than two years. To achieve this goal, the ideal product should have recurring revenues, more than one revenue stream, a short sales cycle, a fast cash conversion cycle, and good gross margins and be quick to market.

Critical questions from investors include the time to market and when you start selling. The breakeven timeline is important to the investor, and this is dependent on cost structure, gross margins, sales cycle, and any new research or development costs. All this information will provide the investor with the path to profitability. An investor will look carefully at the resources required to achieve the successful timelines and milestones with the current financials and the management team.

The Entrepreneur

The fundamental question that entrepreneurs and investors ask themselves is how to define the value proposition of your product to your customer. If the value proposition is not obvious to the investor during the discussion, it will be his first question. A follow-up question by the investor will be "Are you able to continuously add value to the product going forward, and are there new technology advances keeping you head of the competition?" Entrepreneurs need to be aware of whether their solution can be worked around with a new product or are there alternative products that can achieve similar results. Except for medical products, companies like to get their early-stage product out into the market as fast as possible, particularly to test new ideas.

Customers can provide feedback, and changes can be adapted into the next version of the product. Shorter sales cycles and faster cash conversion cycles give the company a strong revenue position to survive the boom-and-bust cycles of the economy. Also, maintaining gross margins from early online sales cycles keeps the cash flow positive and cash is king. By leveraging large distribution channels through financially strong agreements and partnerships, you can strengthen the even flow of your product to the customer. Many frustrated customers wait too long to get products and just cancel their orders. Sometimes, a large promotional budget (social media) is necessary to build "big" awareness of your product if the competition has similar benefits. A good example of this is in the cosmetic industry. It is dominated by large marketing budgets with little product (ingredients) differentiation.

The best way to characterize your product is by defining recurring revenue stream(s): This is important for getting investors interested in your company. The time to getting your product to market and getting your first dollar into the company is one of the parameters for funding companies. Your timeline for breaking even with cash in and cash out of the company is also a benchmark for investors. The entrepreneur should be aware of the product's cost structure, including cost of goods with their margins and the sales cycle timeline. Not only are hospitals and government agencies notorious for being a huge barrier to entering their medical market, but their payment program can be very slow (glacial). Most entrepreneurs are never satisfied with their product. Scientists are notorious for saying "There is always one more experiment or modification before it can go out to the customer." Research and development costs can get out of hand or the product may never get made or never make it to the customer because they are still looking for the perfect widget.

The entrepreneur needs to understand how the product will go from the manufacturing plant to the different channels for distribution to the customers. These agreements or partnerships require both trust and a fair share of the profits so that the company has a reasonable path to profitability within its first two years. This process will require a good balance sheet with reasonable cash conversion ratios and the resources required to be successful with appropriate timelines and milestones. There will be a more detailed discussion of the company's financials in Chapter 13.

The Customer

The customer needs a compelling value proposition to change their buying habits. The customer must be, to a certain degree, unhappy with their current comparable product. Medical products need to be selective and nontoxic. There are very few drugs that can achieve a level of efficacy. The customer wonders if they do switch to your product, will there be a continuous added value going forward, is something better around the corner, or is there an alternative product available? With the rise of Internet shopping (Amazon), most products can be bought online so there is little motivation to buy directly from a local company. Unfortunately, service companies depend on product sales with high margins to keep them in business. Also, the customer wants a faster time to market for the product. Many companies have addressed these issues by creating stores with smaller footprints and limited inventory. The customer can now define the product they want and have the product delivered in one to three business days. The customer does not need to carry the product home; it is delivered to their doorstep. Sometimes, to enhance the shopping experience, a little alcohol is added to make it a special event. We are back to the 1950s shopping model. This maximizes the effectiveness of the entrepreneur and the product and leverages channel distribution with special partnerships.

The Investor

How are you going to make money?

—Angel Investor Philosophy

The fundamental question an investor asks is how do you define the value proposition of your product to your customer? The value proposition must be obvious in the discussion. The investor also wants to know if there is more than one arrow in your quiver (other products in the pipeline). A product with multiple revenue streams is ideal. Does the entrepreneur have new technology to advance the product and keep ahead of the competition? The investor worries that a new product or alternative product will be able to achieve similar results.

The Business Model Template

There are a variety of business model templates available for early-stage to Fortune 50 companies. All templates have a certain set of categories, which include cost structure, revenue, value proposition, key activities, key resources, channels, customer segments, and go-to-market plan. These templates delve into deeper levels of information depending on the company's maturity. The template chosen should be suitable to the age and stage of the company.

- Cost structure includes salaries and administration, sales and marketing fees, brick and mortar expenses (monthly rent), and research and product development.
- Revenue streams include fees, advertising revenue, and payments.
- Value proposition, cost of goods sold (COGS) to margins, time to market? First sales, first dollar, and breakeven point, more than one stream of revenue; increasing size, recurring revenues; sales cycle and cash conversion cycle; leveraging channel players with partnerships; and a clear path to profitability in around two years.
- Key activities, research and platform technologies, define the secret sauce, prototype validation, product to market plans, an outsourcing plan, and the downside of outsourcing.
- Key resources, developing an intimate knowledge of the entire ecosystem in which your business exists, key industry statistics for market leaders.
- Key relationship networks including manufacturing, distribution channels, sales and marketing.
- Customer segments, value propositions, including quality, price, reliability, and experience, and information on which

customers can buy the product, how can we reach those
customers, what must we provide in exchange for their
money, how do we make repeat sales to the same customers,
And how do we add additional revenue streams over time.

The business model needs to secure recurring revenues for the entrepreneur and investor. The customer benefits from the new product with a
better value than competitive products.

Conclusion

The business model is critical for the success of the company. The product
needs to be ready to sell in the market. Product improvements can come
after sales begin and not before entering the market. The target customer
needs to value the product over the competition and be able to afford to
buy the product. The investor needs to know the product, customer, market, and the competition. To lower the risk to investors, the product needs
to be legally protected, the manufacturing process has to be defined, distribution channels have to be confirmed, and the sales and marketing
strategy has to be in place. Answers to the following questions can ease
investor concerns and help mitigate the risk of losing their money:

- Do you need to develop the product?
- How do you make money?
- What are you selling?
- What is the customer buying now?
- How do you get the target customers?
- How do you grow the niche market?
- What do you need to do to manufacture and deliver the product?
- How do you create and capture value?
- Will you make money?

Reflections on the Issues Addressed in This Section

- Does the company have a business that can make money?
- Does your product have a good value for the customer?
- Does the investor make a fair ROI?

CHAPTER 12

The Go-to-Market Plan

Introduction

Is there is a clearly defined company plan to achieve broad market penetration? The plan should provide a well-defined sales strategy. The company needs to establish necessary partnerships with manufacturers and distributors, and also have a sales and marketing plan. A big decision for the company is whether to do this with internal resources or by outsourcing for the go-to-market plan. The customer may need to experience your product before a purchase. The customer reactions need to be understood. The customer should be able to differentiate your product from the competition. There are some investors that like a SWOT (strengths, weaknesses, opportunities, and threats) analysis of the product in the company presentation but there are some business professors that do not think highly of the SWOT analysis. My recommendation is to have a SWOT slide in the appendix of the presentation or modify the SWOT analysis so it does not look like a SWOT table but the information is there for the investor.

Branding

A big issue that faces all entrepreneurs is the need to get your target customer to adopt your product; one of the answers is branding. A simple and repeated message that is easily remembered is what the product needs. In the 2016 national political election, one candidate was effective in branding his political opponents. Unfortunately, that was his only skill set—a lesson learned on how effective branding can be on the customer (or voter). The entrepreneur needs to define their plans for market penetration or their strategy for successfully selling their product to the customer. Investors look for this plan in their discussions with the company and in the company's funding presentation. This market strategy should include a product branding plan, product or service features, packaging features, merchandizing and selling strategy, and the use of the Internet for product messaging (including websites and social media).

Manufacturing

The manufacturing contracts, including any third-party developers or outsourcing requirements, need day-to-day management. Contracts should have timelines, milestones, and goals associated with the manufacture of the product. In my personal experience, we contracted out the manufacture of a set of antibodies for detecting a surface protein associated with melanoma. We were promised it was a routine biochemical process to screen the bacteria and produce large quantities of the antibody. It was promised in a matter of weeks and not more than three months. We received the antibody 18 months later. Ironically, several of our other milestones were equally delayed. Thus, the goal to sell the company took five years and not two years. But we did eventually sell the company. The customers and investors were very patient. Conversely, if we had manufactured the antibodies in house, it would have been four to eight times more expensive but maybe with a shorter turnaround time.

Distribution

The distribution contracts have similar problems as other contracts. Any third-party developers or outsourcing requirements need day-to-day management. The contract should also have timelines, milestones, and goals associated with the distribution of the product. In my personal experience, we contracted out with distributors, and it has been less painful.

Sales and Marketing

The validation of customer sales include the following: sales cycle timeline, generate revenue, the cost of acquiring and retaining customers, customer life cycle, any sales funnel leakage, the marketing funnel, and whether you can grow your market.

Customer

The customer's experience of your product is critical for gaining market share. The customer expects that your product should not have any manufacturing and supply chain issues. The customer needs to be able to afford the product and be willing to pay for your product. During the COVID-19 pandemic, we saw significant disruption of product distribution that frustrated the customers.

Investor

The investor knows your target customer and market. "Will the customer buy your products?" This is the issue for the investor. They also know the barriers to entering your market. Medical products have two issues for the investor: FDA and the slow sales cycle of medical and government institutions. The investor understands the issues for market penetration or strategy for successfully selling their product to these customers. Investors look for the entrepreneur's go-to-market plan in the company's presentation. The strategy should include a sales plan, manufacturing and distribution contracts, and any third-party developers or outsourcing requirements with timelines and milestones.

These are some of the questions an investor will ask the entrepreneur regarding their go-to-market plan:

- Who will decide product branding?
- Which agency has the best reputation for your product?
- What survey data defined the best target customer and sales strategy?
- What are the broad market penetration issues?
- What are the options for third-party developers (QC and QA)?
- What are the manufacturing issues; are they in-house or outsourced?
- What are the distribution partners' issues; are they reliable?
- Who are your service providers and are there issues of value versus cost?

Conclusion

The entrepreneur has big challenges to get their product to market. Their product needs a lot of customer research. The areas of most interest are the following: customer surveys, target customer, beachhead market, branding, manufacturing, distribution, sales, and marketing strategies. The answers to these questions require a strong business network for making a successful company.

The customer will buy your product if they trust you and your company (brand loyalty). The investor wants to know how they will retain customers, grow the market, and maintain the supply chain. The investors network can add value to the company and provide more than just money. The investor will want a short turnaround time for their ROI.

Reflections on the Issues Addressed in This Section

- Does the product have the right brand?
- Does your product attract your customer with the right sales and marketing plan?
- Does the investor know how the product will be manufactured and distributed to the market?

How are you going to generate revenue by your plan of acquisition and retention of your customers?

—Angel Investor Philosophy

CHAPTER 13

The Financial Plan

Cash is king.

—Angel Investor Philosophy

Introduction

If you have the money, you can have the control of the company and make the product sell. One of the biggest killers of startup companies is they simply run out of money.

The CEO has control over the finances, but they are not usually managed properly. As investors, we repeatedly see CEOs underestimate their cash flow; this can causes delays in product development and an inability to pay weekly salaries. Entrepreneurs underestimate the amount of time required as well as the amount of cash necessary to achieve their goals and timelines. Most investors need to support their portfolio companies with bridge funding for the company to hit their milestones.

Many entrepreneurs, especially hybrid entrepreneurs, do not want to spend time on their financial projections and their revenue potential. Why make a five-year projection when you know all the timelines, milestones, and goals will change within 6 to 12 months? Many entrepreneurs know that they could be pivoting their product, customer, or market in six months.

But these projections can tell the investor how the company is performing financially and where the company needs to improve their business model. A good business plan with financial projections clearly explains the company's growth strategy. The company will also need its revenue projections for routine financial reporting for taxes on a monthly, quarterly, or annual basis.

The Entrepreneur

Most hybrid entrepreneurs have worked with budgets in their funded academic research programs. Government funding is one of the most important early-stage financial supports you can get for your research and startup company. It helps your company, and it is equity free for the company. Investors also like National Institutes of Health (NIH) funding in the form of research grants, Small Business Innovation Research (SBIR) grants, and Small Business Technology Transfer (STTR) grants. There are other more expensive types of funding such as seed capital from investors, personal loans, or my most favorite funding source: friends, families, and fools (FFF).

Entrepreneurs have several nondilutive funding opportunities provided by the federal government: The SBIR and the STTR programs are good examples. Innovators can apply for both funding and follow-on funding up to $1 million in grants. These federal agencies have funded approximately $2.5 billion in early-stage funding to entrepreneurs and the regional innovation ecosystem. The National Science Foundation I-Corp is one of the programs to train scientists to become entrepreneurs and help commercialize their technology. Massachusetts Institute of Technology (MIT) has one of the early I-Corp programs that has been successful for postdoctorate fellows looking for alternate career plans. This was discussed in Chapter 1.

> *Any non-diluted financial support for the company lowers the anxiety of investors; the more non-diluted money, the better.*
>
> —Angel Investor Philosophy

Investors will want financial projections for any of these first-round funding sources. If they do not ask for this financial information, you may want to reconsider taking money from them. They would appear not to be a sophisticated investor. This could create problems in the future.

It is important for the company to understand what the startup costs will be now and over the next two years. This information plays a role in defining the potential valuation metric used by investors.

The financial projections should also include the timeline for first sale and when you can achieve a breakeven point (cash in versus cash out are equal). Projection graphs (time versus revenue or versus number of customers or versus products sold) help visualize the data and are necessary for investor presentations. The sales cycle graphs are important for describing the good, better, or best strategy. These data are important: Assumptions are clearly defined. These assumptions should include any revenue sources, the product list price, cost of goods and the margins, the number of customers required to launch the product, the timing of the sales cycle, and at what point should the company break even.

The budget should define the use of funds over time and correlate with income statements (profit and loss), which will include management salaries, technical staff, lawyers, accounts, and a public relations firm if necessary.

A balance sheet will include the financial information over a monthly, quarterly, and annual timeline. This type of information will demonstrate a financial maturity that will give confidence to the investor to carry on discussions with the company.

The term EBITDA (earnings before interest, taxes, depreciation, and amortization) is one of the terms not to get tripped up on by investors.

The Customer

Has your customer validated your business model?
—Angel Investor Philosophy

The customer is looking for a reliable product, a reasonable price, and a product that is better than the competition. A strong financial plan will reassure the customer that the product and company are in stable hands. This can evolve into brand loyalty. My wife does this business analysis for her most important products at home.

The Investor

How is my investment going to be spent (the financials) by the company?
—Angel Investor Philosophy

Investors look for experienced management teams. The company needs to present realistic financial goals and milestones. The company should have a financial statement that is comparable to the industry standards for the product, customer, and market. The company's financial assumptions will be compared to industry standards with recurring revenue streams, growth rates, market penetration, adoption, barriers to entry, competition, customer adoption and closing rates, and sales cycle.

Most investors look for a reasonable financial plan and budget from the company. Investors look at the overhead: Are the operations set to support projections? Does the sales pipeline match the projections? Are the customer adoption and sales cycle reasonable to reach the cash flow breakeven point before they reach $10 million in revenue? Customer cost of acquisition and retention rate is an important factor for an investor's decision to invest. It is common in due diligence for the investor to dig into the company's compensation packages, the Cap Table with the company ownership, and if there are any debt issues or risky financial agreements.

A high pre-money valuation can create a lack of appetite by the investors for a premium stake in the company. If too much capital is required to get a good ROI, the investors believe that they could be diluted in the end. The investors are looking for a clear path to quick profitability. A low pre-money valuation may limit these risks and future dilution of the early investors. Finally, the timelines and milestones must be reasonable.

> *The company's financial statement reveals the maturity of the entrepreneur to the investor.*
> —Angel Investor Philosophy

> *Matching the progress of funding with the milestones and timelines.*
> —Angel Investor Philosophy

> *Managing the money can lead to many unrealistic expectations by the team.*
> —Angel Investor Philosophy

Conclusion

The entrepreneur needs to have control of the company spending and reasonable budget projections. The customer looks for a stable financial company when buying their products. Investor evaluation of the financials is one of their most important topics. They will dig into the company's financial strength and maturity. The financial timelines, milestones, and goals are critical for the investor to get their ROI. A common question asked by investors is: When will the company break even financially?

Reflections on the Issues Addressed in This Section

- Does the company have enough cash?
- Will the customer buy your product?
- Did the investor put enough money into the company?

PART 5

The Ecosystem

Chapter 14. The Incubators
"Your network"

Chapter 15. The Attorneys
"Your protection"

Chapter 16. The Investors
"Your saviors"

CHAPTER 14

The Incubators

Introduction

Incubators, service providers, and investors can make a significant contribution to the business ecosystem. The incubators can facilitate product development for the entrepreneurs. They support the individuals with a network of investors, attorneys, and service providers associated with these incubators. The business essentials offered by these ecosystems enable the entrepreneur to go from concept to product more successfully than if they were on their own.

Government Programs

The university is a major source of patented research. The government has a long history of funding medical research, especially in the Boston area. The government (NSF I-Corp) also supports these adventures with education and applied research funding programs. The National Institutes of Health Small Business Innovation Research (SBIR) and Small Business Technology Transfer (STTR) programs help innovators, entrepreneurs, researchers, and small technology firms. You can apply for funding (between $100,000 and $1 million in grants). The NSF I-Corp is one of the more recent government programs to train scientists to become entrepreneurs. This is an education and cultural challenge for both the program and the scientists. MIT has one of the early I-Corp programs that has shown success after four years and is included in their MIT Venture Mentoring Service (VMS). This VMS program has been in existence for over 15 years and has spun out several similar mentoring programs across the nation. Entrepreneurs need to learn how to access these opportunities. These grants can help fledgling companies. In addition, obtaining these nonequity grants can enhance investor funding opportunities.

Incubators

There are several types of incubators including nonprofits at universities, private for-profit incubators, and accelerator and government-sponsored incubators.

Universities have several forms of incubators. Examples include the IDEA accelerator (idea@neu.edu) at Northeastern University in Boston, the Harvard Innovation Lab, and the MIT VMS program.

For-profit incubators have been modeled after the Y Combinator. They provide seed funding at an early stage of a new venture. Incubators help with startup expenses for an equity position in the company. Twice a year, Y Combinator invests in about 100 startup companies with about $120,000 per company. They have supported more than 1,400 companies over the years.

How much money is necessary to start a company? Some companies may need no more than seed funding. Others will go through several rounds of funding. There is no right answer; funding needs depend on the type of company (technology or nontechnology). The incubator's goal is to get your company through the first phase of funding. This usually means the company can then impress enough investors to raise the next round of money at a larger scale.

An important role of the incubator is to help founders deal with investors and acquirers. They can make introductions for the entrepreneurs. They spend time teaching founders how to pitch their startups to investors or how to close a deal once they've generated interest. In the second phase, they supply not just advice but protection; potential investors are more likely to treat startup companies well if they have incubator assistance.

The government institutions support innovation at the local (cities), regional (state), and federal level. There are government-sponsored incubators at local (Los Angeles Business Technology Center in Altadena, CA) or state level (MassChallenge in Boston, MA). Mentors (investors) and service providers (legal, financial, sales, marketing, and business development) come from all sectors of the ecosystem for help from these programs. Incubators (both university and government) can be at local or state level. One example is MassChallenge (www.masschallenge.org)

where they have created a startup-friendly accelerator. They take no equity and are industry agnostic. They have a competition with several million dollars in equity-free cash awards for their accelerators in Boston, and internationally with access to our corporate partners. To date, 1,211 MassChallenge alumni have raised over $2 billion in funding, generated approximately $900 million in revenue, and created over 65,000 direct jobs. Mentors and service providers come from all sectors of the ecosystem for this program.

This is one of the national and internationally known incubators for creating a healthy convergent ecosystem for entrepreneurs. The Northeastern University student-driven IDEA accelerator is another model for college and alumni entrepreneurs.

In my experience, Mark Lieberman is one of the most effective managers of complex entrepreneur ecosystems for startup companies. The Los Angeles Business Technology Center in Altadena, CA, is another example of a healthy ecosystem. The ultimate success of the entrepreneur is dependent on satisfying the customer with their product and rewarding the investor with a good ROI.

Entrepreneurial Educational Programs

University innovation programs are available as courses, seminars, or guest speaker series. Other formats done by the university and their technology transfer offices include Boot Camps, Hack-A-Thons, Shark Tank competitions, or other competition events for new ventures. In universities, an ecosystem for the entrepreneur is created by education, incubating the concepts with professional mentors and launching the ventures with financial support. Ideally, these programs are open to all associated with the community (alumni, faculty, graduate students, undergraduate students, and staff). Support services can also include specialty clubs for entrepreneurs including legal consults, financial analysis, design options on products, and business models. The mentoring groups come in many sizes and flavors. The concept of attracting experienced business executives into "Venture Mentoring Networks" is common in New England universities. In California, universities draw on investment groups to mentor and evaluate university technology and new ventures.

Investors

Angel investor groups, with a 503-C nonprofit status, work with universities to evaluate and mentor early-stage spinout companies. Their expertise includes legal issues, financial plans, sales, marketing, human resources (finding talent), and business development. These topics are extensively covered in other resources on entrepreneurial ecosystems.

I have worked with investment communities in both California and Boston. The West Coast business culture is very different from the Boston biotechnology community. The biggest differences between these venture communities are the types of ideas that are funded. The funding process, criteria, and the appetite for specific products in Boston are for therapeutics with a high ROI. Within each city, there are cultural and investment priorities for the entrepreneur to overcome. On the bright side, if your team has some affiliation with MIT, you are more likely to get funding in Boston.

How do you fit successfully into this venture network? We will explore these differences in Chapter 16. The good news is that recently, local and regional government–business collaborations are infusing money into the biotech sector. Some noteworthy events include the following: the new initiative in New York City (around $1.1 billion); the Governor of Massachusetts has committed a new round of funding for Boston and the state (around $500 million), and San Diego has been designated the emerging genomic center of the United States (roughly 115 genomic companies, with over 10,000 employees and nearly $6 billion in revenue). Los Angeles, not known for a strong life science community of new ventures, has recently created about 150,000 new jobs with over $1 billion in federal research funding. There has been a coming together of the academic community and the incubator facilities across the Los Angeles basin. This convergent ecosystem has been led by UCLA and has spun out several incubators on and off campus in Westwood: LA Bio Med (Harbor-UCLA) on the South Bay, East LA Bio Science Hub near USC Medical Center and CAL State LA Campus, and in Monrovia near Cal Tech a new incubator, Lab Launch. These new ecosystems have had to overcome geographical distance, traffic, and cultural isolation to emerge with the new vitality.

In this decade, Kendall Square in Cambridge, MA, has developed the largest concentration of biotech companies in the world. The pharmaceutical industry uses startup ventures to test high-risk preclinical research. This offers an opportunity for the investment community to fund early-stage companies with a hope of a high buy out (ROI) from the Kendall Square community.

Conclusion

This is the age of entrepreneurship. With the COVID-19 pandemic impacting job, careers, and lifestyles, starting your own company is much easier than 20 years ago. Government, academics, and the business community have created safety nets for the entrepreneur to enhance the probability of success. It takes an iconoclastic personality to start a new venture, however.

Reflections on the Issues Addressed in This Section

- Does the company have the right network?
- Will the customer have the product available to buy?
- Do the investors know the company support system?

CHAPTER 15

The Attorneys

You can never have enough good attorneys and they are worth it.
—Angel Investor Philosophy

Introduction

There are several types of lawyers that you may need for both yourself and your company. You may need them at different stages of your company or all of them at once. A good attorney can help you as your company grows. These are the types of lawyers you may need: personal lawyer, a patent attorney, and a corporate and commercial/business (mergers and acquisitions) lawyer. As your company evolves, you may need some if not all of them. Be safe and use their skills to protect your assets. Their advice is worth it.

The law is integral to the protection of both the individual and the company. The attorney is an advocate for anyone with a legal issue. Attorneys connect society to the legal system in both adversarial and advocacy positions. Lawyers have a strict code of ethics, and their role is to protect both the law and the rights of individuals. As an advocate, attorneys act on a client's behalf, researching and applying written law.

Conversely, in an adversarial position, an attorney may argue for the law and against you. The practice of law requires a degree from an accredited law school. There are two tiers of attorney jobs. One is a general application of duties that involve advising clients; interpreting laws, rulings, and regulations; analyzing probable outcomes based on legal precedents; developing strategies; and evaluating findings. They must also be skilled in negotiation and interpretation of the law and act as an agent for their client. The second tier includes specialization lawyers that focus on patent law, corporate law, or business law.

Corporate Lawyers

Corporate lawyers serve one client, the corporation, in which they are employed. Small corporations may retain one or two lawyers on staff while larger corporations may have numerous lawyers, each with their own specialty. Typically, corporations like biotechnology companies require the full-time services of a corporate lawyer. A corporate lawyer is also known as a chief legal officer. Their primary objective is to serve the interests of the corporation, not the owners of the business or the officers who run it. In addition to legal counsel, they may also be called upon to provide business advice. It helps to find a lawyer with both a Juris Doctor (JD) and an MBA degree. They may practice other areas of law concerning mergers and acquisitions, trademarks, tax law, bankruptcy, employment, securities, or international commercial law. Their other duties may include negotiating employee contracts, drafting legal documents, reviewing new business relationships with vendors and subcontractors, guiding managers on regulatory and compliance matters, analyzing legal issues relating to proposed products, representing the corporation before administrative boards and court trials, and structuring joint enterprises with other organizations.

Commercial Lawyers

Commercial lawyers are concerned with mergers and acquisitions for your company. Much of their job involves planning for early- or later-stage execution where they work with the principals and try to understand their goals and help analyze risks. From a legal perspective, it's designing a path from where the client is to where it wants to be. Clients want commercial lawyers to do many things including antitrust work or working with industry regulatory bodies. Often there are roadblocks to deals such as special litigation, contingent liabilities, and problems at the target company.

Patent Lawyers

Patent lawyers specialize in protecting the property rights of inventors. They represent inventors during the patent application process and can function as litigators to protect their clients' rights of invention. Patent lawyers (with a college degree in science or engineering) must complete law school and earn their JD. In addition to passing their state bar exam to earn licensure, patent lawyers who want to argue before the U.S. Patent and Trademark Office (USPTO) must pass an additional USPTO licensing exam.

Applying for a patent is a complicated procedure that requires the expertise of a lawyer who is trained to interpret the rules and regulations of the patent process, negotiate contracts, file documents, and provide legal representation to inventors. They conduct searches to ensure that an invention has not been previously represented in the public domain and is patentable. They draft, file, and prosecute patent applications on behalf of inventors before the USPTO. Patent attorneys also provide legal representation in cases of patent infringement, challenges to the license of an invention, and appeals to the USPTO. The field of patent law is complex and by its nature is always evolving. Therefore, continuing education courses are required for patent lawyers to remain up to date with current laws covering patents. A patent attorney will be required to help protect your company's intellectual property (IP), trademark, copyright, or trade secrets. The first question the patent attorney will ask the entrepreneur is "Has the concept been reduced to practice?"

Why an Entrepreneur Needs a Patent Attorney

The patent attorney can evaluate the product and determine if it can be legally protected. The product name, logo, and slogan will also require protection with trademarks or copyrights. The attorney can create protectable barriers for your product to block any competitors. They can also research any competing or alternative technology.

The Investor

The investors look to see who legally represents the company and products. The investment communities are small, and it is important to get well-respected legal counsel that is known to the investors. There will also be several attorneys in the investment group that can make their legal opinions known to the members.

The first set of product questions the investors will ask the entrepreneur will include if the product is a total and unique technology solution. It is important that competitors cannot work around the product solution. The second set of legal questions the investors will ask the entrepreneur is whether there is an MVP and whether the product development has been completed? For the investor, it is important that the product has been validated and the results have been confirmed by external sources. The investor is also interested if the product can solve other problems and have multiple revenue sources.

Conclusion

Having more than one lawyer can always provide you with multiple opinions; at times, it could be more than you may need. Your customer wants to be protected from knockoffs of your product. As noted in this chapter, attorneys cost money, but attorneys ultimately save you money in the long run. Hire the right attorney and listen to their advice. You may someday be sitting across from an acquiring company; you can be sure they are not using a bargain basement attorney to do their deal.

CHAPTER 16

The Investors

Introduction

Investors are not charities.

The team needs to approach the right investors with interest and knowledge of their product. Investment groups usually have specialty areas of interest with product expertise, domain knowledge of the customer, the market, and the industry trends. The investor will evaluate the company presentation, the team's interactions, and the team's problem-solving skills. Investors have a deep knowledge of successful companies and a painful awareness of unsuccessful companies.

The Entrepreneur

The entrepreneur needs to know that there are many types of investors, both national and international. Most investors are of a certain age and gender and have extensive business experience (20 to 45 years). In addition to their domain knowledge, work experience, and education, they have institutional knowledge of entrepreneurs and new ventures. Most investors can review several hundred companies a year through business plans, interviews, company screenings, presentations, or due diligence.

Investors involved in this many yearly evaluations can quickly see patterns likely to result in funding. The entrepreneur should be aware of the types of investors and investment groups. Finding the best fit between the investor's domain expertise and the entrepreneur's product offers the best path for success.

The investor's educational background can also be important. An undergraduate education at MIT in Boston was an important criterion for joining the Pasadena Angels in California. Other educational institutions on the East Coast were accepted, but with a little bit of reluctance.

Woman investors have recently been actively recruited into the investment community. A national women's investment group called "Golden Seeds" funds companies with at least one woman on the management team. I have worked with this group. They have brought a large number of quality deals to our investors. Golden Seeds has also done some of the best due diligence on their companies as compared to other investment groups. The percentage of women in investment groups range from less than 5 to 25 percent. This is still a small number, but it has significantly increased in recent years. We also had an active program to recruit women into our investment group; women now represent roughly 25 percent of the membership of the Pasadena Angels.

Investor's Domain Expertise and Network

When an entrepreneur presents to an investment group, there are 20 to 50 members with extensive industry experience, investment experience, and a deep network that they can draw on to understand the technology and the business. The type of questions the investors ask will reflect their domain experience. That will tell you a lot about their business experiences and network. Before presenting to investors, you should do research on the domain experts and reach out to your network to connect with these types of investors.

An Entrepreneur's Relationship With Investors

There are investors that have lost their investments when the entrepreneur was less than honest. They can easily walk away from any deal; listen and learn. Investors are looking to see if they can trust you with their money. Your network and reputation are critical for getting funded.

The entrepreneur's reputation is their most valuable asset.
—Angel Investor Philosophy

The Criteria for an SEC-Accredited Investor

There are many people that can qualify as an SEC-accredited investor. In 2010, there were over 350,000 U.S. citizens with liquid assets over $1 million. In 2015, there were only about 8,000 angel investors in roughly 250 SEC-accredited angel groups. They invested over $23 billion on new and bridge company funding. In 2015, about 300 venture funds invested approximately $28 billion in new ventures. In 2000, there were about 1,500 venture funds. Because of the economy and a low ROI for their clients, the number of venture firms has significantly reduced. In a new twist, the pharmaceutical industry has moved aggressively into the venture fund community with about 900 deals by corporate ventures with approximately $8 billion in seed funding for new life science companies. Support for this research, however, does not provide them with any rights, such as the right of first refusal, on the technology or patents.

One of the dangers for the angel investor is that the CEO can turn their venture into a lifestyle company. The CEO draws a very high salary and sometimes has little incentive to grow the company. The investors cannot get their investment back with any significant return. Thus, an exit plan for the company and investors is very important.

The Types of Investments

Friends, Family, and Fools

The first type of money an entrepreneur will likely see is from friends, family, and fools (FFF). They can invest up to $250,000 to validate the concept and build the prototype. This type of funding can help make your prototype. An example of this type of funding was when parents invested a few hundred thousand dollars in their son's (CEO) new venture (Amazon) in the early 1990s. Today, the parents are billionaires, and their son is still with the company.

The Angels

The second type of money the entrepreneur will see is "smart" money. The company needs to have identified the target customer and market.

The concept has been reduced to practice with a prototype. The Angels (Series A) take preferred series A stock only, they do not like common stock, and they are taking a big risk in the early venture. The investors use their own money. More deals are done when the stock market is having a good run. Investors like to take some of the stock market profits off the table and invest a portion into high-risk early-stage ventures. The entrepreneur submits their package (their presentation and one-page summary of the company) on the investor's website.

The investors that have domain expertise review and sometimes mentor the entrepreneur to make the deal more fundable. Experienced investors may take a board seat. The investor funding ranges from $1 to $5 million for Series A companies. Deals can be syndicated between other local angel groups and venture capital groups. This is more common in California and occurs less in Boston, MA. In my 20 years of investor experience in California, I've dealt with two Los Angeles area investment groups: the Pasadena Angels (www.pasadenaangels.com) and the Tech Coast Angels (www.techcoastangels.com). In Boston, MA, a new group for investors and entrepreneurs is the Sky Ventures model (www.sky ventures.com).

Venture Capitalist

The third type of investors is *venture capitalists (VCs)*. The VCs invest in the growth stage of the product and company. They use other people's money. They want and get referrals. The deals are more mature and fundable, have their own management teams, and narrow focus on funding areas, and VCs typically take a board seat and provide funding ranging from $1 to $20 million. They can bring on their own management team and may want to flip the company to a corporation for a quick ROI.

Corporate Venture Funds

The fourth type of investor is the industry venture funds such as Johnson & Johnson, Novartis, Pfizer, and several other pharmaceutical companies. They provide seed funding and co-invest with angels and VCs but they do not take the deal lead.

Corporate Deals

Late-stage corporate deals are common in the pharmaceutical industry. The products have a lower risk of failure in the clinic and can give the new venture the highest return. The new company has taken all the risk getting the product to market. The pharmaceutical companies have the cash and sales and marketing expertise to scale the sales in their pipeline.

Crowd Funding

The advantage of crowd funding your company is that it can be fast and easy money if it is the right fit for the investor. But the potentially easy money comes with several disadvantages: They are nonaccredited investors, the government requires several company reporting statements per year, and the CEO and the company are exposed to litigation by the crowd-funding investors.

Note that SEC investors in angel groups will not usually invest in crowd-funded companies because of their exposure to litigation by the crowd funders. In angel groups, members invest as individuals only and not as a group. The members invest their own money at their own risk. Most angel groups have rules where they cannot sue other members over investments if the deal goes bad.

Syndication of Deals

Investors in California and Boston (East Coast) syndicate deals co-invest at local, regional, and national levels. The Angel Capital Association (ACA) has about 250 angel groups in their membership and syndicate deals nationally. It is very common for most companies to need follow-on funding.

Investor Deal Flow

Angel investors call the process of funding companies the "deal flow." The entrepreneur comes up with their concept or solution to a specific problem. They do the research and find that their idea is novel. There are many sources of investment. Investors are always looking for new entrepreneurs, new ventures, new technology at universities, or in incubators for new products and companies.

The smart money from angel investors is the next step in the funding process for the entrepreneur. The investor will require a working product and a defined target customer. Angel investors can invest anywhere from around $100,000 to about $1 million. With this funding, the entrepreneur can validate the market, pivot if necessary, and scale the business. The investors can syndicate the deal with other investment groups to gain traction and momentum with about $2 million from local, regional, and national angel groups (ACA). The next step in the deal flow is the scale-up for sales and marketing by a venture capital group(s) to a sum of approximately $1 to $25 million, depending on the product, market, and competition. If all goes well, the entrepreneur and investors can look forward to a merger and acquisition or initial public offering (IPO) (depending on the economic climate).

The Investor Deal Process

Capturing the Interest of an Investor

If the investor is curious about your new venture, they will ask questions. Investors like to know how you got involved with the topic and what made you start digging into the problem. Investors like to see how you think and the assumptions you made when developing your solution. What issues are still unanswered? An interested investor will ask you where they can go to get the best information on the topic. Another favorite question they often ask an entrepreneur is: "If you could start over again tomorrow, what would you do differently?" If the investor asks you these types of questions, the good news is they are interested in you and your company. Here is how you can follow up with the investor process.

Finding the Right Investor for Your Venture

The first question that the entrepreneur should ask an investor is if their network has expertise in your product. If not, ask if they know an investor for your specific product. In the Tech Coast Angels, the San Diego network focused on life science and biotech startup companies. The Los

Angeles Tech Coast Angels network focused on digital and media ventures. The Pasadena Angels, with their technology expertise, focused on patent-protected technology. Sky Ventures in Boston specifically focused on health care and life science. Although these investors do sometimes look at other technology ventures, their sweet spot is their member domain expertise.

Elevator Pitch

This is sometimes the first contact you will have with investors. Make good eye contact with the person. You have about one to two minutes to get them interested in your idea.

You need to explain who you are and why your team can take the product to market.

If the investor asks you questions or needs clarification on a topic or issue, you can move into a more detailed description of you and your company. In two to five minutes, you can address the problem and your solution, the importance, and the disruptive nature of the solution to the competition. The investor may follow up in an effort to better understand your product. They will be interested in knowing the stage of development, if you have outside verifiable results, if there are any significant improvements or cost reductions, or if the product can solve other problems. They will also be interested in any competition and the status of your product with patent protection (i.e., reduced to practice, novelty, any barriers to entry, or your unique insight).

If the investor is still interested in your proposal, they will follow up with financial questions, such as target customer and the size of the addressable market. They will need to understand your business model and its value proposition and the sales cycle. The investor will be very interested if they move into your "go-to-market strategy" (branding, manufacturing, sales, distribution, and market strategy). Finally, they will ask you your exit plan: Either grow the company or get acquired at some stage in the product development.

An experienced investor can get to these topics in less than five minutes. They have heard thousands of ideas and proposals over the years. They know how to quickly evaluate the entrepreneur, the product, the customer and market, and the company. If the entrepreneur had all the answers, there would be no need to seek investor help and mentoring. For the investors, it's more than just the money but also mentoring and making a company successful.

The Investor Funding Process

Prescreening

If the investor has a positive response to your pitch, they will recommend that you submit your proposal to the investor's website for review. On average, the investment groups that I have been associated with over the years receive about 25 to 50 proposals a month. This also has a seasonal variation with September and January having the highest submissions and July and August (the summer months) having the slowest submissions. Investors need their vacation time: They enjoy their time off.

Screening

The second step in the funding process requires a small group of investors (15 to 30) to meet monthly and evaluate the top companies (4 to 6) out of about 25. Some of the companies do not fit the criteria of the investors, such as the product is not a technology company that cannot be protected by patents. Investors do not like to invest in bowling alleys or local pizza establishments. Occasionally, a nontechnology company may get funded due to a fast ROI but, in my experience, only one such company was funded by investors out of approximately 300 technology companies.

Company Presentation

The third step is the company presents at the formal member monthly screening meeting. The company gives a short 10- to 15-minute presentation to investors with around 10 to 15 minutes of questions and answers. The investors look for key topics in the presentation. The team's track record and domain experience with the product, and customer, market, and venture experience are critical for getting funded. Investors want to know if the product is protected by patents. The product needs to solve an important problem and gain a large market share. The customers need to want your product over the competition. The product will have to overcome any barriers to entering the market and any adoption issues by the customers.

The most important criterion for evaluating a company is how they will make money. A clear description of the business model is essential with reasonable financial projections and a go-to-market strategy. The investor is looking for an exit that will provide a reasonable return (2 to 10 times) on investment in a timely fashion (within 5 years). The investors look for a team with the ability to pivot if the company stalls in their progress on timelines, milestones, and goals. The investor looks carefully into the team's management expertise, track record, synergistic interactions, their coaching ability, their passion, and most of all their integrity. There will likely be 25 to 50 members with domain experience of the product out of about 100 members. Those members attending the meeting will vote on which company should move forward into due diligence.

Sometimes the companies that do not make the cut are asked to address certain issues and then invited back to the screening session. Often, an investor will mentor the company and can spend 6 to 12 months working with them before presenting again to the investor group. The investors watch very carefully the dynamic interactions of the team before, during, and after the investor presentation.

Conclusion: The company should present to the investors. It has made a sound and plausible argument for commercial viability. If its claims are valid, it could be an attractive angel investment.

An Entrepreneur Can Turn Off an Investor (Honesty Is the Best Policy)

The company's message needs to be clear and simple. You need to get the investors interested in doing a deep dive into your company. These are several red flags to the investor:

- Does the founder listen to the investor's questions?
- Is there too much information on the slides?
- Is there too much science in the presentation?

- Where is the competition slide?
- Is there a lack of expertise on the team for the product, customer, or market?

Be aware that older investors can be visually impaired. It helps to use a larger type size and only three to four bullet points per slide. You can do a deep dive in the question and answer period or a one-on-one after the presentation. The investor looks for the personality and character of the entrepreneur during the presentation. Are there energy, leadership skills, vision, integrity, and humility about their knowledge (academic, science, or medical expertise)? These investors have seen hundreds if not thousands of presentations by entrepreneurs and have seen the outcomes of their careers and their companies. They have deep institutional knowledge that can help founders and new ventures succeed.

Investors are human and can have a bad day or week or month. Be aware, no one is perfect. You, your product, or your company could provoke an unpleasant memory or bad experience. Calmer heads usually prevail in meetings with investors. Be cheerful, pleasant, and show that your personality is good enough to be around 10 to 14 hours a day.

Some of the turnoffs for investors are as follows: The product is not important enough for the customer. If the product is pitched as "patent protectable" or if there is limited patent protection, most investors will stay away from the deal. If the product cannot be differentiated from the competition, it will be difficult to capture new customers or get customers excited. This will lead to adoption rate issues and barriers for the product to gain market share. The investors look for expert endorsements and real third-party validation of the entrepreneur's product. Financials with unrealistic business models and go-to-market strategies can quickly turn off investors. If the customer acquisition and retention plan and the product's price point are unrealistic, this can lead to customer erosion. If the company has too high a pre-money valuation and lacks any premium offers for the investors taking early risk with the company, this could be a turnoff for investors. The big fear for investors is the potential for a long-term or delayed exit. The investors may find it hard to visualize future buyers with the current product. The investors will not get a big enough ROI and other deals have better upside, and faster and bigger returns. This is a common problem when investors compare a life science product requiring FDA approval and a software as a service product for their investment. The investors see too much capital required for the company to achieve an exit or the first investors will be diluted out of the future deal.

Finally, a huge red flag will be if the company has a weak presentation, such as missing critical points or lacking credibility of the product, customer, market, or financials. These types of mistakes reflect the founder's lack experience or mismatched team and leadership issues.

Due Diligence

The last step is a due diligence meeting with the company if there is enough interest among the investors. This usually means a minimum of 10 investors. Alternatively, these deals can be syndicated with other local, regional, or national investment groups.

One of the criticisms of angel investment groups has been the length of time it takes to get funded. It sometimes takes several months (6 to 12). But this is a two-way street; the entrepreneur needs to provide the documents for due diligence but sometimes the investors need to speed up their process. The due diligence process can be difficult, time consuming, and a challenge to both the investor and the entrepreneur. The initial impressions of the entrepreneur and their company should resolve a few issues for the investor. The product should solve a significant problem and the product should fit in the investors' comfort zone. The entrepreneur needs to make a good first impression either on his pitch or at the prescreening.

If the company's presentation goes well with the investors, then there are several phases of due diligence. In the first phase, the experts for the investors will evaluate the team, their technology, the distribution, and revenue model. Investors draw on their outside network to further validate these topics and the company's reputation. The second phase involves an analysis of the product's strengths, weaknesses, opportunities, and threats (SWOT). The competitors need to be defined as well as other technology that can work around the product and patents. The investors will also do a web search for the name of the company, the product, and known or unknown competitors. Investors draw heavily on their network for this information.

The final phase of due diligence involves legal issues, financial analysis, debts or loans, their Cap Table, and the term sheet. This due diligence process can take as short as one week (unusual) or as long as several months. It depends on both sides of the table being prepared and the documents ready for review. When I sold my company, we had a 600-page document in triplicate for the investors to review. Now, thanks to Drop Box, most of the due diligence material can be downloaded electronically for ease of use.

Due Diligence Issues

Issues can occur when the management lacks credibility and are closed-minded. One of the first qualities that investors look for in entrepreneurs is coachability. Investors do not waste their time on difficult entrepreneurs. They do not want to work with entrepreneurs who miss critical points in the due diligence process such as timelines. Other due diligence issues include:

- The influential investors (domain experts) are negative about the company.
- The company has skeletons (issues) that may or may not have been disclosed.
- The product has competition with other solutions or alternative products.
- There is a lack of expert endorsement and validation by outside parties.
- The technology is too immature and there is still too much "invention" required before it can become a product.
- The technology does not have enough differentiation to get a patent or compete with other products.
- The customers are not compelled to buy the product and there is a long sales cycle.
- The biggest challenge for the product is a customer behavior change to buy the product.

Another due diligence issue is there is no compelling story for the VCs to come into the deal if future funding is needed. The exit is too long with the company's timelines and milestones. This could cause a long delay in an ROI or the CEO could create a lifestyle company. The biggest fear of investors not getting their investment return is if a CEO has a well-off salary and does not want to go or sell the company. There are pre-existing agreements that are harmful or expensive for the new investors to justify. Other issues for the investors are shareholders that are disruptive, family members, friends, or former employees.

So how does the investor say they have no interest in funding your company? Often they will just say nothing to the entrepreneur, which can be very frustrating. If you persist, the investor can respond by saying that the company is not a good fit for their investors, or you need more progress on your product (6 to 12 months) before we can review you again, or they need a lead investor before they can invest, or your valuation is too high. Another strategy the investors use is when they will not fund you outright but offer you a small investment, "a tranche," to help you achieve a big milestone. This is not the best option for an early-stage company. I have experienced all these responses and they can be very discouraging. Angel investors tend not to do this too often because they need good will in the entrepreneurial community and they can also play a mentoring role for early-stage companies.

Term Sheet

A term sheet is a document of good will, a memorandum of understanding. Funding occurs when all parties agree to the term sheet. This is usually the most difficult discussion between parties. Therefore, it is necessary to have good lawyers that know the investor process. It can speed up the deal and the entrepreneur can get funded sooner. The Pasadena Angels funded one company, Microfluidics from Salt Lake City, UT, for about $500,000 in less than a month. This was an exceptional case. The company was well run, they had all their due diligence documents in order, and the product was well received by the experts. They were coachable and listened well.

In a term sheet, investors want protection for their investment and the company to succeed. That is a difficult compromise for everyone.

In dealing with an early-stage venture, it is difficult to put a value on future earnings. Some investors like a convertible note to the next round that can offer principal, interest, and a maturity at a discount rate. There can be a conversion price cap with an automatic conversion or an optional conversion. Not everyone is happy with this, but it does satisfy most people in the deal.

One of the challenges for investors on a term sheet is the company's pre-money valuation and the justification of the investors' premium for getting in early on the deal. The investors use convertible notes or preferred stock but never take common stock.

The investors need to protect themselves in the future with pro rata rights and antidilution clauses in the term sheet. The term sheet must also be aligned with acceptable terms now and in the future with other investors and venture funds. Liquidation preferences are common for the investors to get at 1× but sometimes they can get a better deal for the wrong reasons. Be warned.

The deal should be free of back debt, payables, and any cap issues beforehand. The legal support from the investment group should be available at capped fees and with the use of templates with experienced lawyers well known to the group. Both sides need to avoid complex conditions and know that each side can deliver what is expected of them in a timely fashion.

Both sides of the table should not compromise on key deal points and prevent any of the individuals from "falling in love" with the deal terms. For the investors, it helps to have a designated document reviewer on the team that can keep the ball in play and keep the right perspective. The entrepreneur needs a very experienced attorney for the deal. Someone that is comfortable doing investment deals.

Now that the entrepreneur has their term sheet and funding, the fun begins. The company needs to start looking for its next round of funding and, at the same time, move the product timeline and milestones forward. If the angel investors are well connected, they have a pipeline and track record with venture firms to get follow-on funding.

There are different relationships between the angel groups and venture funds on the West Coast versus the East Coast. In southern California, there has been a longer tradition of angel investment for over 25 years with a more diverse funding portfolio. There have also been more opportunities to syndicate deals with other angel groups as well as venture firms. There are several reasons for this collaboration: The angels over the years have developed a better due diligence process, better term sheets, and better mentoring that is more in alignment with standards in venture firms. In addition, there have been stronger interpersonal relationships and trust between the two investment groups that have been beneficial to all involved, including entrepreneurs.

Investor Goals

Investors need a fast exit and a healthy ROI. This will allow them to invest in more deals. Most deals today take 3 to 10 years to mature with a 2× to 10× return. Many studies on investor deals have shown that they need to do at least 10 to 20 investments to break even and get a good ROI. You can see now why most investors are interested in helping entrepreneurs by mentoring them. Most angel investment groups are considered a 503C Nonprofit Educational Group for the internal revenue tax issues.

The angels only invest as individuals, not as an organization. That is why the group is tax exempt. In addition, for educational purposes, the members give talks at the business schools of local universities, judge business competitions, and have students attend the monthly investor screening sessions.

Conclusion

The entrepreneur needs to know their investor and the expertise of the investor group. You need to find the right fit between your company, your product, the mentor, and the investor. The entrepreneur needs to know that investors are not a charity organization. The entrepreneur should be honest with themselves: If your company was perfect, you would not need investors.

The investor needs to connect with the entrepreneur at an intellectual and emotional level. They need to understand the novelty of the product, customer, and market. The investors, once they have committed to supporting the entrepreneur, need to bring their network and investors to the table to make the company successful.

Funding companies is a convoluted and time-consuming process. Both parties need to work together for a smooth and rewarding experience.

Conclusion

It is the questions that you ask, not the answers you give that can be the most helpful.

—Peter Drucker

The entrepreneur's road map to success is through a supportive network. Partnerships with investors and satisfied customers are the key to entrepreneurs achieving their goals. In the American culture, good failures are considered good learning experiences, unlike in other parts of the world. As in evolution, innovation seeks out and adapts to the best product (phenotype) in their environment. The ecosystem (institutional knowledge) supports growth of ideas into commercially viable products. The entrepreneur's character will guide them over the ups and downs of the product development adventure.

Innovation is like evolution. New ideas can take hold in an environment where the entrepreneur adapts to the needs of the customer and is supported by the investor. These relationships can form a very stable stool if everyone works together. Supportive services (service providers, government institutions, incubators, accelerators, university entrepreneurial programs, gate keepers, and finding talent) can enrich entrepreneurial ecosystems.

The hybrid entrepreneur needs to meld the two cultures of science and business together. The culture of science and its vocabulary can make businesspeople very nervous. The business culture and its vocabulary can make the scientist very nervous.

The lawyers make everyone nervous. The hybrid entrepreneur has the potential to lower the anxiety of all their partners. Language, personalities, and cultures can limit interactions in a company and limit the success of a team. Conversely, strong levels of respect between the players can create a successful company. In my experience, companies fail because we do not understand the language, process, and culture of these diverse groups. It is my hope that the journey through my book will enlighten all three groups to make a stronger stool.

What makes a successful company and limits the failure rate? The team has good character (integrity) and has a domain track record in the field. The data and product have been validated with the target customer. The company is well funded. The business model (customer and market research) and financials (revenue streams, sales cycle, breakeven point, and funding needs) show a commercially viable product. The strategies to achieve external funding are reasonable for an angel investment with successive rounds of financing. The deal risk is realistic.

Words of advice:

- Your reputation is your biggest asset.
- Be honest and be fair.
- Network with people you like and trust.
- Please stay away from the riffraff.
- Do not burn your bridges behind you.
- Try to be a little lucky.

Entrepreneurship Is a Team Sport

This book can help entrepreneurs understand the process of creating successful ventures. Successful companies exist in a supportive ecosystem. Business students, entrepreneurs, and hybrid entrepreneurs should now understand how to work convergent ecosystems. An entrepreneur's journey is a team sport. Success is dependent on understanding the needs of the customer, the role service providers, and investors.

Hopefully, this book will help you increase your odds of funding and launching successful businesses. For the hybrid entrepreneur, taking your science or technology and making a product is like the process of evolution; you need to test and adapt to the changing environment. The entrepreneur's innovation needs to adapt to the commercial environment to survive and thrive. The knowledge you have gained from this book will help you find the right ecosystem for your product along with an encouraging network of entrepreneurs, customers, service providers, and investors.

APPENDIX

The Food and Drug Administration

Is your product pure, safe, and efficacious? The three conditions needed to get a drug approved by the FDA.

Introduction

Products that require FDA approval need greater attention in managing timelines, milestones, and barriers that might affect getting the products to market. The FDA requirements for early-stage life science products (therapeutic, diagnostic, medical device, and natural products) scare some investors but not the Boston investors. The role of the FDA is to protect the consumers with safe, pure, and efficacious products (www.fda.gov).

Medical Products

Nonhealth care investors are weary of the FDA because of the effect of milestones and timelines for getting the product to market. However, with an FDA-approved product, there is a better chance of seeing increased profits and being acquired.

In Boston, there is an appetite for licensing out therapeutic candidates from the biomedical community. The investors have a pipeline from the laboratory to a new business venture to validation of the drug candidate to licensing of the product to the pharmaceutical industry in Kendall Square, Boston, MA.

The Entrepreneur

Entrepreneurs need to practice due diligence and address any regulatory-related barriers for their product. FDA experts are usually hired as consultants to help shepherd the product through the regulatory steps. The regulatory process has high probability of success in a realistic timeline. Where the company's success is dependent on patents or other IP ownership rights, it needs to take all necessary steps to obtain such protections.

The Customer

FDA approval gives confidence to the consumer about the safety of the product.

The Investor

Some investors are weary of the FDA because of the effect on the company's milestones and timelines. In Boston, there is an appetite for licensing out therapeutic candidates from the biomedical community. The investors have developed a strong pipeline from the university research programs to the pharmaceutical industry. These new ventures are then supported by the industry for fast track FDA approval and domain expertise for helping obtain IRB, regulatory, and FDA approval with realistic timelines for successful monetization of the drug.

Conclusion

You will need to prove to the FDA that your product is pure, safe, and efficacious. The efficacious rule can be a little ambiguous as seen in several FDA-approved products. The FDA sets the criteria for approval with a defined clinical study. The parameters that the company needs to be aware of for approval of their product are the following: the number of patients required to validate the study and the successful end points of the study.

About the Author

Dr. Kevin J. Scanlon received his PhD in molecular biology at the University of London. Dr. Scanlon's academic achievements include coauthoring 139 scientific articles and 9 medical books. He was a Leukemia Society Scholar and won the Paul Martini Medical Research Prize in Germany. He was cofounder and coeditor of the Nature Journal *Cancer Gene Therapy* and president of the International Society of Cell & Gene Therapy. Dr. Scanlon also holds seven issued U.S. patents. At Berlex-Schering AG (Berlin, Germany), he was responsible for the genomic and cancer programs in the United States, Europe, and Asia. As CEO of Melanoma Diagnostic, he sold his company to Myriad Genetics. When chairman of the Pasadena Angels, he was identified by *LA Techweek* as an individual impacting the Los Angeles Business Community on a significant scale. He was also executive member of the Tech Coast Angels in Los Angeles and investment advisor to Sky Ventures in Boston.

Index